THE CFO YEARBOOK

THE FINANCE CAREER BUILDER'S GUIDE TO THE C-SUITE

2021

THE CFO YEARBOOK

THE FINANCE CAREER BUILDER'S GUIDE TO THE C-SUITE

2021

CFO THOUGHT LEADER BOOKS, 2021

"It was on the financial side that the last necessary key to decentralization with coordinated control was found. That key, in principle, was the concept that if we had the means to review and judge the effectiveness of operations, we could safely leave the prosecution of these operations to those in charge of them."

—Alfred P. Sloan Jr., *My Years with General Motors*

PAGE 75

One of the things... is to create an increased level of understanding of the relationship between what drives revenue and cost.

—Matt Ellis, CFO,

Verizon

67. **Hilla Sferruzza**
CFO, MERITAGE HOMES

68. **Amir Jafari**
CFO, REPUTATION.COM

69. **Michael Borreca**
CFO, LYNX FRANCHISING

70. **John Bonney**
CFO, HARNESS

71. **Gordan Stuart**
CFO, UNIT4

72. **John Cappadona**
CFO, SCHOOL OF ROCK

73. **Will Costolnick**
CFO, HIRE DYNAMICS

74. **Jody Cire**
CFO, ALLCLOUD

75. **Matt Ellis**
CFO, VERIZON

76. **John Nguyen**
CFO, KYRIBA

77. **David Wells**
CFO, ENDRA LIFE SCIENCES

78. **Anders Fohlin**
CFO, MEDIUS

79. **Matt Borowiecki**
CFO, BIOFOURMIS

80. **Jeff Epstein**
BESSEMER VENTURE PARTNERS

81. **Ashim Gupta**
CFO, UIPATH

82. **Dennis McGrath**
CFO, PAVMED

83. **Dave Jones**
CFO, VROOM

84. **Ray Carpenter**
CFO, XANDR

85. **Laurie Krebs**
CFO, RED HAT

86. **Ivor Macleod**
CFO, ATHERSYS

87. **Shane Hansen**
CFO, PLANFUL

88. **Sinohe Terrero**
CFO, ENVOY

89. **Alyssa Filter**
CFO, CLARI

90. **Jason Peterson**
CFO, EPAM SYSTEMS, INC.

91. **Mark Sargent**
CFO, WESTHAVEN POWER

92. **Inder Singh**
CFO, ARM

93. **Angiras Koorapaty**
CFO, REVERSINGLABS

94. **Matt Hagel**
CFO, FRESHLY

95. **Bennett Thiemann**
CFO, APPLICASTER

96. **Steven Springsteel**
CFO, BETTERWORKS

PAGE 101

Everybody has to work together because everybody has a piece of the puzzle and we must make sure that we're collectively doing the right thing for the customer.
—Marsha Smith, CFO, Siemens USA

FOREWORD

I was a first-time CFO, sitting in the office of my boss, Roger King, cofounder and chairman of King World Productions. King World was a New York Stock Exchange–traded company that had rocketed to success as the distributor of the hit TV shows Wheel of Fortune, Jeopardy!, and The Oprah Winfrey Show.

I told Roger about an idea to help our largest customer, the Capital Cities TV station group. Roger said "Great idea!," picked up his phone to call Larry Pollock, the CEO at our customer, and told him the idea. The time that elapsed from me telling Roger to Roger telling Larry was less than 3 minutes.

What did I learn from Roger that day?

First, Roger was close to his customers. Very close. He took advantage of every opportunity to engage with them, help them, and check in with them.

Second, Roger was fast. If he liked an idea, he acted immediately.

Roger was also one of the world's best salespeople. He painted a vision for his customers of how our shows could lead into and out of their local news programs, lifting our customers to #1 ratings in their cities, with higher market share and higher revenue and profits.

When Oprah became a spectacular ratings and financial success, Roger and our team developed a companion talk show starring the motivational speaker Les Brown. At investor meetings, Roger would tell investors, "Les Brown is going to be the next Oprah Winfrey." Then I would give our financial presentation, advising investors to wait to see Les Brown's ratings before they changed their financial forecasts.

Investors appreciated both of our roles. They liked seeing Roger's passion for television and for his star performers. And they were confident when I balanced Roger's enthusiasm with a commonsense approach that treated every new television show like a brand-new start-up business, with an exciting potential but a statistically high rate of failure.

Roger was the visionary sales leader and source of inspiration; I was the analyst and practical manager. Together, we formed a powerful combination.

Continued...

After King World, I went on to become the CFO of DoubleClick, Nielsen's Media Measurement Group, and Oracle. I have served on the boards of directors of Priceline/Booking Holdings, Twilio, and Kaiser Permanente. I joined Bessemer Venture Partners, where I work closely with the CFOs of our fast-growing portfolio companies. I've met hundreds of CFOs and heard their stories.

My friend Jack Sweeney has collected 100 of these CFO stories in this exceptional CFO Yearbook. If you're a CFO—or are on the CFO path—you're in for a real treat because here are our stories. Enjoy!

- Jeff Epstein
Former CFO of Oracle, Operating Partner, Bessemer Venture Partners

INTRODUCTION

About 10 years ago, I was named editor-in-chief of a print magazine for finance executives, a tour of duty that proved to be both disastrous and transformational professionally: "disastrous" because the business model that sustained print journalism was about to collapse and "transformational" because this collapse finally forced me to look beyond print journalism.

My goal in going forward was to develop an information resource for senior executives and business leaders. Still, I had no idea of what type of resource I was going to develop and which group of executives I wanted to serve.

That's when I came upon this observation in Peter Drucker's memoir Adventures of a Bystander: "Yet while he was universally admired throughout the company and known as a truly wise person, most managers wanted as little to do with him as possible. They simply could not understand a word that he was saying. He was dependent on the CEO to translate him."

Drucker's comments were directed at General Motors' historic CFO, Donaldson Brown, the finance leader who had paired up with legendary GM CEO Alfred Sloan to build the company that came to represent the modern American corporation for most of the past century.

If not for Drucker's harsh assessment of CFO Brown, I may have kept reading—but his words triggered something within me. I put down the book and made this note: "I want to help finance and accounting executives connect with others by helping them to shape and share their professional narratives."

What came to me was the notion that in order to connect with broader numbers of stakeholders, many finance leaders were in need of a narrative reboot. In short, they needed to begin explaining themselves and their career experiences in a way that larger numbers of executives could relate to and would find more engaging.

At the same time, it occurred to me that mobile technologies could play a big role in the reboot. I was not yet familiar with the podcasting world, but I felt that if my information resource could feature the actual voices of business leaders, we could shed more light on each leader's emotional intelligence.

As I drilled down on my idea, I became convinced of two things: first, that a narrative reboot would benefit few business leaders more than CFOs, and second, that few forms of media were better suited to sharing narratives than podcasting.

Continued...

At the same time, to help more people discover the podcast, I found an outlet for my dormant writing skills as we began publishing companion articles about our CFO guests in part to please the search engine gods—but also to better amplify some of what was being shared.

Our CFO guests expressed their enthusiasm for our modest dispatches and even urged us to consider a printed collection—hence The CFO Yearbook.

Our 2021 edition—just like the one before it—has but one mission: to inspire CFOs and aspiring finance leaders to advance their own strategic thinking and extend the reach of their thought leadership beyond their organizations.

– Jack Sweeney
Editor
The CFO Yearbook, **2021**

IT'S THE NARRATIVE THAT MATTERS

GUEST CFO
LANNY BAKER
Eventbrite

When it comes to time management, finance leaders tell us that it's often easier for them to manage time offsite than inside the traditional office environment, where calendar appointments and consecutive meetings can swallow up entire days.

Still, few CFOs have shared with us as novel a time management solution as that of CFO Lanny Baker.

"I have always parked in the farthest parking space that I can find in the lot," explains Baker, whose comment leads us to picture an executive emerging from a sea of minivans and sport coupes.

Says Baker: "I've done this as like a time set aside for me, as I walk into the building, to think about the people that I'm going to interact with, and as I walk out of the building, to take stock of every interaction that I've had with people throughout the day."

However, Baker's comments expose something bigger than a time management best practice, additionally highlighting a favorite theme of his involving finance and personal interactions and communications.

As Baker sees it, finance professionals are at risk of spending too much time with the numbers and not enough time with the narrative or not enough time spreading the narrative. Here's where personal interactions and relationships are critical to an executive's development into a leader. "It's not about the numbers," says Baker, whose parking lot ritual is not without risks. "I always tell my team, 'Be careful—I will have meetings with you in my head, and I may have said things to you in my head that I may later think we've talked about, but no, you weren't there.'" ∎

CFOTL: What are your priotities as a CFO over the next 12 months?

Baker: Here at Eventbrite, my priorities are to bring focus and simplicity. We just went through our planning experience for 2020. We started with 12 different strategic initiatives, and I'm happy to say that eight of them wound up on the cutting room floor. We've got four that everybody is really focused on. These four initiatives had 20 subprojects, and these, too, have been dialed down to four. We're just bringing focus and clarity and simplicity.

"ONE OF OUR PRIORITIES IN THE FINANCE TEAM IS HELPING THE COMPANY MAKE THE RIGHT INVESTMENTS, TRACK THESE, MANAGE THESE, AND GET THE PAYOFF."

I teased the team in our flash report. On the 57th page, we put a little note which said that the first person to read the page and call Lanny Baker would get dinner at the restaurant of their choice. That was three months ago, and the phone still hasn't rung. This was just my way of showing the team that some of the complicated reporting that we were doing just wasn't making a difference. Nobody's looking at it, and that's why I'm trying to bring some simplicity and focus.

📱 TO LISTEN

All of this is in support of allowing the company to drive long-term growth. One of our priorities in the finance team is helping the company to accelerate growth, make the right decisions, pick the right priorities, make the right investments, track these, manage these, and get the payoff. ∎

WHY IT'S TIME FOR BI TO TURN THE PAGE

GUEST CFO
MOHIT DASWANI
ThoughtSpot

When Mohit Daswani stepped into the CFO office of Sunnyvale, Calif.-based ThoughtSpot in January 2020, he ascended to something more than just another finance leadership position inside a SaaS start-up.

Daswani was joining a special class of CFOs distinguished by their ability to communicate a vision that connects not just with investors, but also with other CFOs. This is a cohort widely visible within the realm of business Intelligence, or BI, the space where finance leaders frequently shop for new technologies and tools to analyze their business data while surveilling the messaging of BI's latest class of CFO thought leaders.

From the perspective of ThoughtSpot, which raised $248 million in late-stage funding last August, the world of BI is now colliding with the world of artificial intelligence and moving the competitive state of play from visualization to real-time data delivery.

"This is just a very different offering and value proposition from the current state of BI," explains Daswani, who was previously the head of finance and strategy at payments company Square, Inc.

"This is about giving business customers not just a static dashboard, but also the ability to query the data in real time and create a natural language search on the front end," adds Daswani, who quickly lists Walmart, 7-Eleven, Celebrity Cruises, and Hulu as ThoughtSpot customers.

For some BI watchers, Daswani's arrival is a feat of fortunate timing, perhaps matched only by that of those executives who once occupied the CFO office at such companies as Cognos and BusinessObjects, the pioneering BI technology companies that many credit with having helped to launch the first big wave of wide-scale BI tool adoption.

Then came Tableau, with its powerful visualization tools that indoctrinated even more CFOs into the ranks of the BI faithful. Acquired by Salesforce last June for $14.6 billion, Tableau was a property whose sale became a milestone that few BI watchers could ignore. Add to this Google's purchase last year of Looker, another visually driven developer, and it's clear that visualization is now in BI's arsenal, says Daswani.

"If I'm a CFO or marketing lead, I no longer have to enlist a data scientist to go build a query or dashboard for me," notes Daswani.

"We're talking directly to that decision-maker and company and saying, 'How do we make your life easier? If you're a CFO, you need to understand what's going on with working capital, because you're managing your cash flow. Let us make it easier for you to do that directly,'" reports Daswani, who these days is busy standardizing work flows and procedures.

"The Valley is building a lot of great companies right now. I've met with many of them over the past few years, but ThoughtSpot stood out for me in multiple dimensions," says Daswani. ■

CFOTL: Tell us how you achieve "buy in" with employees, investors and board members.

Daswani: It's always a two-way street. I have to straight-shoot with people and identify the trade-offs that would need to be made. Are we going to put that incremental dollar into marketing or into product? Let's bring the stakeholders around the table and make this decision. Or do we want to decide that instead of growing margins right now, we're going to invest more in the business because we think that this is the right thing to do. And then you go and explain this to your board and whoever your stakeholders are, whether you're a private company and it's your VCs or, if you're public, it's obviously your investors. But let's make sure about the story, and then let's have our key things that we're going to measure to show that we're being successful with that story. ■

SCAN ME

📱 TO LISTEN

A WINDOW INTO THE FUTURE

GUEST CFO
ANNA BRUNELLE
Kinestral Technologies

 sked to reflect on those experiences that she feels prepared her for a finance leadership role, a cash flow statement quickly comes to mind for Anna Brunelle, CFO of Kinestral Technologies.

Only months into her first industry finance job, Brunelle was tasked with preparing her company's cash flow statement, and she didn't like some of what she discovered about the business.

"NOT KNOWING ANY BETTER, I WENT TO THE CFO AND CEO AND SAID, 'HEY, HAVE WE EVER THOUGHT ABOUT TRANSFERRING SOME OF THE ELEMENTS OUT OF THESE BUSINESSES?'"

"I realized that there were a couple of businesses that the company had acquired a few years earlier that had some elements that were kind of dragging down our profitability," explains Brunelle, who after digging a little deeper and more closely studying the businesses realized that the areas negatively impacting profits frequently involved certain offerings of recently acquired European businesses that offered limited cross-selling potential.

"Not knowing any better, I went to the CFO and CEO and said, 'Hey, have we ever thought about transferring some of the elements out of these businesses?,'" recalls Brunelle, who even today as a CFO appears somewhat surprised by her early-career assertiveness.

She continues: "I say 'I didn't know any better' because I was only two months on the job, and I didn't know that there was probably more of a process of going through your manager to do this. Instead, I just said, 'Hey, has anybody thought about this?'"

According to Brunelle, only days later she was boarding a plane to Europe to help execute on her suggestion and sell off underperforming assets and parts of the business that were perhaps not as profitable as was desired or in line with the company's future direction.

"I got on a plane having never traveled to Rome before, not knowing any lawyers or accountants or bankers there. I worked through getting an introduction to a banker to help us package these busnesses and find buyers and then getting an introduction to an attorney who could help us with the local Italian law and how to structure the contracts for these transactions," says Brunelle, who credits the resulting deal-making with helping to distinguish her as an executive "who gets things done."

"They were relatively small transactions," she adds. "I think that one was about a $10 million sale and one was about a $30 million sale. But for me, so early in my career, this was the moment when I realized that finance was the way to open the door to being part of the more exciting strategic business conversations." ■

CFOTL: Tell us about your top-of-mind metrics.

Brunelle: Because we have a fairly complex business, we have to have a pretty well thought out strategic plan and metrics. By "complex business," I mean that we have the Taiwan factory and we also have research and development teams here who are creating new products as well as innovating on existing products to make them less expensive. We also have a chemistry division that applies what you would think of as the ink that causes our windows to darken; they do the chemical formulations and composition here. We have the software division in Salt Lake City. So, multiple elements have to come together in order for us to be successful. ■

IDENTIFYING THE LEVERS OF EFFICIENT GROWTH

GUEST CFO
JOHN EVARTS
Mediafly

Ten years or so ago, the expression "never waste a downturn" became a popular maxim among business leaders who viewed the economy's downward spiral as an opportunity to trim waste and restructure portions of their businesses. The expression also summed up the mind-set of a unique class of executives who, despite a bleak hiring environment, viewed the period as being potentially transformational for their careers.

Such was the case with CFO John Evarts, who entered the downturn as a CFO for a not-for-profit and exited as CFO of Mediafly—a small content asset management company that in the coming years would open a new growth chapter by answering the demand for more compelling content in sales enablement.

"WHEN I SHIFTED FROM THE NOT-FOR-PROFIT AREA INTO 'START-UP LAND,' I WAS FORTUNATE TO HAVE THIS AMAZING OPPORTUNITY TO PLAY A MORE STRATEGIC ROLE"

"From late 2008 to 2009, there were some challenges inside the not-for-profit sector, so I started looking for an opportunity to broaden myself beyond the not-for-profit realm—I was comfortable in taking that risk and making a bet on myself," explains Evarts, who had originally transitioned into the not-for-profit sector from the world of investment banking and has also taken on the title of COO during his Mediafly tenure. "When I shifted from the not-for-profit area into 'start-up land,' I was fortunate to have this amazing opportunity to play a more strategic role and determine how to deploy resources in a more strategic way." ∎

CFOTL: Tell us about a finance strategic moment of insight...

Evarts: Our first opportunity for mergers and acquisitions was really what I would say was a watershed moment for me. I had never had the opportunity to pursue an acquisition before, and I needed to figure out for myself what a framework would be in order to determine whether this was a good one or not a good one. It's very different from what's in the textbooks. When you get into the actual practical matter of pursuing an acquisition, you need to be very disciplined in how you look at it, how you think it through. We had to come up with this construct that we call our 100-day plan. When I started thinking about how to make that construct and 100-day plan—what we call "one Mediafly"—it really started driving home the point that culture is critical.

The reason why we're acquiring this company is so that not only do we get the benefit of the products, but also we get the benefit of the really great people who are on the team. We were able to get this 100-day plan around M&A as a way for us to think about and philosophize about this "one Mediafly" concept, which is, for example, the way that we look at how to source the capital that is necessary and we begin to think about how people work within the organization. So, it's not only how many resources we need in order to acquire this company, but also what does the construct in the comp model look like afterward? What is the expectation of revenue production that's going to come out afterward?

Then, over time, you get to the point where you're also talking about culture and its impact. What do you think about when more than 50% of the company is outside of the Chicago headquarters? What do you do? How do you think about remote work? This, for me, was kind of an "A-ha!" moment, once we got to this concept of "one Mediafly." ∎

SCAN ME
📱 TO LISTEN

ENERGIZING YOUR ENTREPRENEURIAL

GUEST CFO
STEPHEN GRIST
Bohemia Interactive Simulations

 t was back in 2002, Stephen Grist says, when he first punched through a surface of rigid assumptions to grasp the innovative levers that would propel him into the ranks of strategic CFOs.

At the time, Grist was the CFO of Viatel, a technology company whose management and sales teams were eagerly seeking to reestablish the company's footing along a growth path after having recently emerged from a Chapter 11 bankruptcy.

With its bankruptcy in the rearview mirror, the company advanced with an unbridled appetite for growth—but one that was perhaps lacking in long-term vision.

Says Grist: "The existing business managers were so focused on 'Take that hill!' and 'This is our business, and this is the path that we're going down!' They just were not capable of identifying the disruptive risks."

Having already logged a string of seven-day weeks to hasten Viatel's exit from bankruptcy, Grist might have found it easy to applaud the sales team's mounting tactical wins and provide diligent governance. Instead, he engaged the company's general counsel, and together they approached a number of bankers in order to "add on" some small Internet businesses that could quickly diversify the types of services that Viatel offered to its small to midsize customers.

According to Grist, Viatel at the time was struggling with "The Innovator's Dilemma"—a phrase referring to disruptive competitors first coined and used as the title of a popular text by Harvard professor Clayton Christensen.

"You're so caught up in your vision of the company that you're not really capable of identifying where those disruptive risks

are affecting the company as they come in from different directions," says Grist, who looks back at 2002 as a turning point for both Viatel and his CFO career. Moving forward, Grist has entered new CFO roles as a disruptive risk expert tasked with questioning assumptions.

"Every time I've come into a company, it's been like, 'Okay, it's time to do the long-term business plan'—but you've got a different view of the world, so you can ask all those questions," says Grist, who since Viatel has served in a string CFO roles for both founder-led and VC-backed companies.

Says Grist: "As the CFO, you bring your experience to bear and you identify risks as you build the next year's budget or the long-term model from really being in a position to question assumptions." ■

CFOTL: Tell us about Bohemia and what sets its offerings apart in the market today...

Grist: Bohemia is in a really interesting space. What I was particularly attracted to was the types of customers that Bohemia serves, which are some of the world's largest military organizations and prime contractors. We do so in a very disruptive and innovative way, using software to completely change how people might think about training. When I saw government budgets obviously coming under greater pressure, and then the idea of having soldiers running around in a field and all of the costs that this entails when compared with doing it in software, it was clear that this was a very exciting market for a company to be in.

Looking at behavior, we see that many of our relationships with our primary customers have been for an average of 10 or 11 years or so, with, for example, the U.S. Army and the U.S. Marine Corps. We've only been in existence for about 15 years, so this spoke to me of a very deep customer engagement. A very successful product makes the customers themselves successful, and in fact that's been the case. ■

SCAN ME
TO LISTEN

WHEN HIS LEADERSHIP MOMENT ARRIVED

GUEST CFO
BRIAN WENZEL
Synchrony

I t was roughly 10 years ago when Brian Wenzel realized that his coveted and time-tested career path inside GE Capital had become somewhat fogged over.

He was not alone. Somewhere between the economic downturn and GE's headline-grabbing restructuring, Wenzel and his career-building colleagues had seen their traditional corporate career ladder begin to disappear in a haze of uncertainty.

"I learned a lot through this time that helped me to develop as a leader. I'm not sure that I enjoyed things quite as much in '09 or '10, but this really was a situation that honed my skills to perform in a difficult and adverse situation," says Wenzel, who at the time was CFO of the retail card unit—a position that he would keep after GE Capital split off its retail lending arm to form Synchrony Financial in 2014.

"I HAD THIS NORTH STAR THAT I WAS FOLLOWING FOR MY CAREER."

At the time, Wenzel recalls, he shared his future CFO aspirations in a meeting with Synchrony CEO Margaret Keane and then-CFO Brian Doubles.

"Hey, listen, my goal is to be the CFO of this company—I love this company" are the words that Wenzel remembers using to demonstrate his commitment to Synchrony and in part to restore the career path that had for a short but trying time seemed to disappear.

"This journey took me a long time, but along the way, I had this North Star that I was following for my career. I was creating different experiences that built out my

capabilities and skills in order to be ready for the CFO moment when it came," he explains, adding that he had been given the "Deputy CFO" moniker in 2018.

"In any crisis, whether an economic one or just a crisis within your company, rallying around it and not being afraid and instead saying, 'Listen, I want to lead through it,' is tremendous," says Wenzel, reflecting on the mind-set that he adopted during the financial crisis and has assumed at other times during his career.

He adds: "I think that when you're inside large companies like GE or others, there's this whole thing about how to climb the stairs to get to the top. You want to be able to get up those stairs as quickly as possible and not fall."

Asked what lessons he may have already learned as a CFO, Wenzel responds that while he originally thought that he might find questions from sell-side analysts "nerve-wracking," he has since found thorough preparation to be an easy remedy. Still, when it comes to his new, outward-facing responsibilities, Wenzel says that one nagging thought is always top-of-mind: "I represent 17,000 employees, and you want to perform at your best when you represent them in public." ∎

CFOTL: When Synchrony split off from GE, did certain business functions need to be rebuilt?

Wenzel: The processes that we have had to develope are at the core part of our business. We had to build everything from scratch. Even the processes for very mundane things like benefits, and paying people, as well as some of the regulatory reporting. All had to be built up. But we did take a process from GE. And it was a very good process in the credit risk world. Traditionally, you go out and get underwriting scores from credit bureaus, you look at the data, you kind of put a score together, and you say "yes" or "no."

We have developed this process where we're able to take multiple data elements into consideration, including what we get from our partners. ...We look at our 80 million active cardholders. ∎

SCAN ME
📱 TO LISTEN

BUILDING YOUR P&L CULTURE

GUEST CFO
SCOT PARNELL
DailyPay

We are nearly at the end of our interview with Scot Parnell when we ask him to explain what led him to accept the CFO position at DailyPay, a company with a pioneering technology inside the human capital management realm.

This is a question that we had asked a little earlier in the interview, but this time we want to know what other factors may have contributed to his decision. Although Parnell has already put forth a compelling explanation of DailyPay's unique offerings, he is happy to share a bit more with us.

"THE CFO AND CEO HAVE TO DO A VULCAN MIND-MELD TO MAKE SURE THAT THEY'RE NOT ONLY OF THE SAME MIND, BUT ALSO ABLE TO WORK TOGETHER AS A TEAM."

"This role was absolutely fascinating. I was at a place in my life where I could take some risks, and I also think that I've got some runway here. For me, it was too important to be absolutely excited about going to work every day. It makes me a better leader. It makes me a better husband and father when I find fulfillment in what I'm doing," explains Parnell, whose response suddenly widens our lens to a better view of what sets apart his latest CFO career chapter from earlier ones.

"As I sat back and looked at what I wanted to do next, this just felt like I could get more excited about it and put more of my soul into it, so that's what I did," he continues, while expressing a sentiment that many finance leaders experience but frequently resist acting upon.

Having spent the past 20 years as a finance leader in large enterprise organizations, Parnell has observations about the entrepreneurial realm that undoubtedly signal a fresh enthusiasm that few CFOs can muster—and particularly those who may have built their careers as start-up CFOs but over time have become more integrated into their surroundings.

Nonetheless, when it comes to CEO–CFO relationships, Parnell's comments are suddenly strikingly similar to those of a broad swath of his CFO peers: "The CFO and CEO have to do a Vulcan mind-meld to make sure that they're not only of the same mind, but also able to work together as a team and provide each other balance and support." ∎

CFOTL: What comes to mind when we ask for a finance strategic moment?

Parnell: A great example was when I first got to the Student Loan Corporation (of Citigroup). It was very revenue-focused. There was a lot of attention paid to top line growth, and the balance of power and focus was on it. At the same time, it was pretty clear when I walked in, being the new guy, that the company was underwriting a disproportionate amount of risky loans, and in the student loan space, it is not good for the company or the borrower to be in a risky loan. A cultural shift was required. I had to gather information and perspectives from everybody involved, all the stakeholders, and I had to model out what was going to happen over time, depending on how we made different decisions. Eventually, I was able to convince people that we needed to change.

We developed risk-based pricing. We reinforced the credit standards. We were able to get better pricing across the board, such that riskier accounts were charged more and less risky ones were charged less than originally had been the case—which means that we won on volume and on rate when we went to market with the revised products. ∎

SCAN ME

📱 TO LISTEN

A UNICORN'S CFO KEEPS RISK TOP OF MIND

GUEST CFO
MICHAEL TANNENBAUM
Brex, Inc.

pon being named CFO of Brex, Inc., in 2017, Michael Tannenbaum joined a realm of accomplished finance executives whose average age is 20 years greater than his.

This is not the first time that Tannenbaum has advanced beyond his professional years, so the label of "whiz kid" has long since lost a little of its adhesive.

However, as a CFO's son—who recalls reading the WSJ at summer camp—Tannenbaum has observations about his CFO role that demonstrate more circumspection than one might expect from your average C-suite Millennial.

Tannenbaum joined Brex after having occupied a VP of finance role at SoFi (Social Finance, Inc.), a fintech company best known for student debt refinancing. "I decided that I would join them as the first employee of Brex," he recalls, referring to Brex's cofounders, Henrique Dubugras and Pedro Franceschi.

"When I came on board, we were not in a garage but in the CEO's house, and from there I became involved in operations and ran marketing and business development," says Tannenbaum, who also focused on raising capital. Most recently, Brex raised $200 million in debt from Credit Suisse (December 2019), following a similar $100 million deal from Barclays earlier in the year.

However, rather than recap the savvy mechanics behind Brex's capital-raising, Tannenbaum habitually highlights the firm's efforts to establish Brex as a risk management brand. "Ultimately, we at Brex need to be known for our brand of risk management because we are asking customers to trust us with their money," explains Tannebaum, who views enhancing Brex's risk brand as a 2020 priority. ∎

Q&A

CFOTL: Tell us about a finance strategic moment.

Tannenbaum: At Brex, pretty early on, I was kind of familiar with the banking landscape from when I had been in investment banking. The group that I had been in actually served regional banks, so I did a lot of regional bank mergers and acquisitions. Then, at SoFi, I had built a lot of relationships with regional banks. I think that when you start in fintech, there's always this belief that you're competing with big banks. That was a lot of the marketing positioning of my former employer, SoFi, but at Brex I saw this opportunity to partner with banks because I was familiar with the card landscape. At least in the commercial card space, outside of the Big Four banks—Wells, Citi, Bank of America, Chase—there are very few financial institutions that actually issue corporate cards.

"TECHNOLOGY IS CHANGING SO MANY INDUSTRIES AND CREATING LOTS OF OPPORTUNITIES, AS WELL AS DISRUPTION AND UNCERTAINTY."

I decided that even though we were a small company, subscale, no one had heard of us, banks might want to partner with us because they themselves were fighting their own battles with the Big Four issuers, as well as American Express. So we partnered with a number of banks very early on in a way that most people would think was not possible and was unusual. Ultimately in financial services, brands, particularly with regard to trust and stability, are super important. Today, what's exciting is that technology is changing so many industries and creating lots of opportunities, as well as disruption and uncertainty. At Brex, we need to be known for the brand of our risk management because ultimately we're asking both customers and other businesses to trust us. ∎

SCAN ME

📱 TO LISTEN

A FINANCE LEADER WITH A TASTE FOR SALES

GUEST CFO
MAHESH PATEL
Druva

aving already answered the majority of questions, CFO Mahesh Patel was in the homestretch of our interview when he shared something that sets him apart from most of our finance leader guests: If he were entering the workforce today, he would set his sights on becoming a sales leader.

"There's a thrill of the hunt as we work with customers and try to find out how we win and why we win," explains Patel, who, having raised more than $200 million in equity financing at Druva, doesn't hesitate to remind us that when it comes to positioning a business, CFOs can be counted among their company's top salespeople.

Still, his remarks likely reflect more a recurring restlessness than any legitimate career regret, for it was arguably this same drive that led this one-time aspiring tax attorney to shelve a law degree in order to enter the finance lane inside a number of entrepreneurial businesses.

"It's atypical of CFOs, but if I could wind back the clock, I'd seriously think about it," observes Patel, who credits the entrepreneurial realm with allowing executives to reap satisfaction from their own creativity and willingness to collaborate to achieve success. Adds Patel: "As we've just been talking, I received a call from one of our sales reps. I have an open door policy and always say, 'Just ask ....'" ∎

CFOTL: What comes to mind when we ask for a finance strategic moment?

Patel: When I joined the organization, we were selling all of our solutions, all of our technology, in an à la carte fashion. When my engineering organization built a new feature, it was handed to the sales organization as "Here's a new feature that you can go sell." We effectively had an à la carte list of 10 to 20 solutions that you could buy. I started to recognize that none of these new value-added features actually added significant extra ARR or bookings or dollars or revenue to us. Meanwhile, I'm investing in these solutions, but there are only two ways in which it would make sense for me to continue to build them if they're not resulting in new revenue: They have to start driving new, additional revenue, or they have to allow me to win more often—and it didn't seem to me like these were driving additional win rates either.

"THESE NEW TECHNOLOGIES THAT WE WERE BUILDING WEREN'T GETTING VALUED— THERE WAS NO VALUE BEING ATTRIBUTED TO THEM."

It became a bizarre situation where I felt like we were actually commoditizing ourselves. These new technologies that we were building weren't getting valued—there was no value being attributed to them. So I, my CEO, even a board member, worked together on how we think about the pricing and packaging of our solutions. We went from selling 10 to 20 different solutions to actually bring it down to just three. We started bundling every solution, and bundling multiple solutions into one. This made our sales organization start thinking about selling value—not just augmenting solutions to get a deal over the finish line, but now selling value and understanding how to go to an organization not with the base use case, but actually the whole portfolio.

As we did this, our customers started to understand what Druva could offer as a company, versus point solution after point solution. We started becoming a platform, and how this manifested itself was that we actually started seeing revenue-per-account increasing. ∎

EXPOSING THE GROWTH AND RISK TRAJECTORY

GUEST CFO
KEVIN JACOBSON
LogicGate

 tep inside CFO Kevin Jacobson's office at LogicGate, and there's little question that you'll think you've entered a realm where growth and risk are often two sides of the same coin.

In fact, LogicGate's fast path to achieving "product market fit" was no doubt shortened by early customers who today wield a similar growth/risk mind-set.

"I TELL OUR TEAM THAT GOING FORWARD, WE ARE GOING TO BE BREAKING RECORDS ACROSS EVERY METRIC IN EVERY QUARTER."

Four-year-old LogicGate, a provider of governance, risk, and compliance (GRC) software, now expects its workforce to expand to 170 employees before 2021.

Says Jacobson: "I tell our team that going forward, we are going to be breaking records across every metric in every quarter."

With yet another year of impressive growth behind LogicGate, Jacobson says that the company's foundation has been firmly laid for a new growth chapter to be built.

"We've grown significantly since last year, and my role is now about keeping a vigilant eye on what matters in this new context, this next stage of growth," he explains. ■

TO LISTEN

CFOTL: As a CFO, do you have a philosophy or mind-set when it comes to managing risk?

Jacobson: There are many buckets of risk that our customers are trying to deal with. There's IT security risk. There's general business risk in terms of many different things, whether it's your cash position, your competitive strategy, things like that. We're a small and now ever-growing team, as we've continued to layer on how we manage risk at the company. For example, one of the hires that we've made this year is an assistant general counsel, who is leading the legal risk of the company. We sign a lot of contracts with customers and vendors, and there's inherently risk that needs to be mitigated when you're doing that type of business. We also brought on an information security leader, who is keeping an eye on all of our information security programs, policies, and procedures so that we can tell our customers, "You know, we're going to take care of your data as if it were our own and protect it."

These are some of the things that are top-of-mind from a kind of truly operational risk standpoint: the legal risk and the information security risk. Inherently, there are other business risks, too. For example, for a venture-backed company, there's financing risk: Are you going to be able to raise your next round of financing? That's something that we've been thinking about basically since I got here, and closing our series B was kind of our near-term path for mitigating that financing risk.

I think that the ways in which we think about risk are pretty holistic. We've addressed them in many different ways, whether by bringing someone onto the team who we feel is really going to help us appropriately manage a risk or during things like strategic planning. We're going through our fiscal year 2020 strategic planning process right now. Thinking ahead, as we continue to grow and get to a different scale than we were this past year, what kinds of challenges and risks are we going to experience? How can we mitigate against them now? ■

GROWING YOUR TEAM'S KNOWLEDGE BASE

GUEST CFO
RAJ DANI
Ping Identity

B ack in the early 1990s, with both feet firmly planted on an auditing career path inside Price Waterhouse's Tampa, Florida, office, Raj Dani decided to take a detour into the accounting house's M&A advisory practice.

Over the next few years, the one-time auditor began providing deal-makers with financial and operational due diligence on their future mergers and acquisitions.

"I became focused on cash and EBITDA generation, the strategic value of two enterprises coming together, and how you drive synergies and value for shareholders," explains Dani, who says that his segue into M&A opened the door to experiences that have never for a minute led him to reconsider the auditor's path.

"IT WAS JUST A MAJOR LIFE LESSON ON HOW TO TREAT PEOPLE WHEN YOU'RE INTEGRATING TWO CULTURES AND HOW TO BE RESPECTFUL OF PEOPLE AND THEIR DIFFERENCES."

Dani's jump into Price Waterhouse's M&A advisory services also allowed the former auditor to gain international experience when the M&A practice shortly thereafter transferred him to Zurich, Switzerland.

It is perhaps little surprise that Dani's post-PW career has also involved both M&A and Europe.

Looking to enhance its European operations as well as its new ventures portfolio, Jabil Circuit enlisted Dani to help lead its corporate development efforts from its Milan, Italy, office.

Reflecting on his different M&A roles overseas, Dani says that "it was just a major life lesson on how to treat people when you're integrating two cultures and how to be respectful of people and their differences."

Today, as CFO of Ping Identity, of Denver, Colorado, Dani credits his early-career "M&A detour" along with his budding relationships inside the private equity realm with having helped advance him into the CFO office. ∎

CFOTL: What are your priorities as a finance leader over the next 12 months?

Dani: In terms of our priorities at Ping Identity and my own as a finance leader overall, my first priority is making sure that I continue to work from a team perspective, to work on progressing my team's knowledge base and experience, and to thus give them greater career path opportunities. If you don't think long-term about your people, they're thinking long-term about themselves, and they want to make sure that they're partnered with a company and leader who have their best interests in mind. This is not something that most leaders think of just off the top of their head as their number one priority, but it is absolutely all about the people for me because without these people, we would get bogged down very quickly. We hire well, we train well, and we make sure that they're getting out of the company just as much as the company is getting out of them. You cannot have this equation be out of balance. So, I really do prioritize the people-centric initiatives from a business perspective.

As we mentioned on our last quarterly call, we're now really leaning into designing sales and marketing investments to monetize some of these product investments. A lot of my focus will be on the operations of the business and making sure that our new CMO is successful and getting what he needs to continue to elevate our brand. ∎

SCAN ME
📱 TO LISTEN

THE INNER WORKINGS OF CUSTOMER SUCCESS

GUEST CFO
SUE VESTRI
Greenphire Inc.

 n the past, Sue Vestri has told friends that she has achieved CFO success by routinely working herself out of jobs.

Vestri is not alone. Certainly, many of her finance leader peers have helped to create some exciting M&A deal-making chapters only to be "written out" of the newly merged business's future script.

"Being put out of a job isn't necessarily a bad thing, as one opportunity can open the door to the next—or at least it has for me," says Vestri, whose latest career post as CFO of Greenphire opened up just as her previous role as CFO of Artisan Mobile of Philadelphia was closing down with the sale of the company in 2015.

"I was thinking that I'd actually take the summer off, but that didn't happen," says Vestri, who remembers being contacted by a recruiter about Greenphire, which was yet another Philadelphia-area company that had recently been acquired and was looking for some local C-suite talent to beef up its management ranks.

Along the way, some of the local deal-making impacting her career has involved out-of-town acquirers.

Such was the case back in 2010, when Dell acquired Boomi, a Philadelphia-area technology developer specializing in integration technologies. At Boomi, Vestri had advanced into a finance leadership role just as the giant technology provider from Round Rock, Texas, came knocking.

Says Vestri: "With Dell being public at the time, the whole process and early discussions had to be kept very confidential." In light of Dell's concerns, Vestri says, Boomi looked for space off-site and ended up renting a hotel meeting room for a period of months.

"The process involved maybe a half-dozen people from our side, but there was literally an army of executives from Dell," she recalls. ■

CFOTL: What customer measures have become top-of-mind?

Vestri: I think that everyone tries to measure customer service and customer support in some way. In the past, we have done customer surveys and implementation after implementation periodically throughout the year. It's always challenging as to who actually responds and how you disseminate the information and make any use of it. We still do these types of things, but recently we've actually gone out and done some user forums where we've sat in the room with some of our users. To be honest, not all of the feedback was good. There were some pretty harsh critics at some of these forums that we did. It was really actually good for us to hear this, and it's driving a different strategy for us going into 2020.

"FOR US, A BIG DRIVER OF REVENUE IS GETTING CLIENTS WORLDWIDE TO USE THE SOFTWARE IN THE WAY THAT IT WAS INTENDED."

We rely on our partners to do a lot of the training on how to utilize our software, and we're finding that this may not be the most successful way to get people up and using it. For us, a big driver of revenue is getting clients worldwide to use the software in the way that it was intended. We are spending a tremendous amount of energy on understanding our clients and what it's going to take to make them happy. ■

SCAN ME

📱 TO LISTEN

SCALING R&D TO DRIVE GREATER GROWTH

GUEST CFO
DAVID BURT
ServiceTitan

Y ears from now, when finance leader David Burt is reminiscing about his varied career chapters, you might imagine a captivated listener politely interrupting the veteran CFO with the question, "Excuse me, but what exactly was your profession?"

This is a query perhaps more likely to be asked of veteran CFOs than other seasoned business leaders, in light of how finance leaders are less tethered than others to any one industry or opportunity throughout their careers.

Such is the case with Burt, who, as CFO of ServiceTitan, is busily applying his patchwork of business and industry experiences to the multibillion-dollar residential home services industry.

"BURT RECALLS THAT BACK IN 2012, NETFLIX REALIZED THAT THREE COMPANIES— DISNEY, NICKELODEON, AND THE CARTOON NETWORK—WOULD SOMEDAY SOON WIELD A POWERFUL ADVANTAGE "

Turn back the clock 20 years, and you'd find Burt helping companies expand into China as a Bain & Company consultant based in Sydney, Australia, his original home. Ten years later, you'd find him evaluating digital media acquisition targets as an investment banker with JP Morgan. Only 8 years after that, you'd see him roaming the frontlines of the streaming wars while serving as co-head of corporate development for Netflix.

Today, Burt views his finance leadership role as being not unlike that in an earlier chapter as a strategic advisor, when he sought to help empower management to be more outward-looking. He says that finance executives "oftentimes get boxed into just looking at the internal aspects of the company."

To highlight his point, Burt recalls that back in 2012, Netflix realized that three companies— Disney, Nickelodeon, and the Cartoon Network— would someday soon wield a powerful advantage inside the realm of children's content as more consumers turned to streaming.

"I asked myself, 'If I were sitting in the FP&A teams for those companies, what would things look like?' I realized pretty quickly that this meant that we as a company would need to begin investing in original content much sooner," explains Burt, who says that up until that time, Netflix had been focused on developing content mostly for more mature audiences, with shows like Orange Is the New Black. ■

CFOTL: What are your top-of-mind metrics?

Burt: The first things that I look at on a weekly and monthly basis tend to center on the fundamentals. Once we're in the door with a customer, there's an opportunity for us to provide additional services that might add additional recurring revenue. This growth is really important because it allows us to forward-invest into areas of R&D, sales and marketing, and so forth. We are of a certain size today, but we have aspirations to be much, much bigger, and as we grow, we are enabled to do more and more for our customers more efficiently because we can scale our investments in R&D across a larger base.

The second big area that I like to focus on is our unit economics. It's important to look at not just the numbers and the financials, but also what might be underlying indicators of key metrics in this third area. ■

SCAN ME

▢ TO LISTEN

OPTIMIZING YOUR PIPELINE'S VELOCITY

GUEST CFO
GREG WOOKEY
Boulevard

Inside the world of retail businesses, Greg Wookey's CFO career has advanced down a path that parallels the sector's growing appetite for more sophisticated software.

Such was the case roughly 10 years ago, when he stepped into the CFO office at Mindbody—a firm whose well-known software helped fitness centers across the country to manage the demands of their clientele—and such is the case today, as Wookey serves as CFO of Boulevard, a SaaS developer whose offerings are specially tailored to high-end salons and spas.

"WE SAW THAT THERE WAS AN INABILITY OF SALON OWNERS TO CONNECT EFFECTIVELY WITH THEIR CLIENTELE."

This arena—in what Boulevard and other software developers commonly refer to as "appointment-based retail"—is where Boulevard now hopes to help salon and spa owners to achieve a more sophisticated and aesthetically pleasing customer booking experience.

"We saw that there was an inability of salon owners to connect effectively with their clientele, so this was about making booking appointments and integrating payments easier so that salon owners could accept payments more easily," says Wookey.

Meanwhile, Wookey is keeping a close eye on Boulevard's own customer engagement activities. "We actually have very good metrics in terms of the size of our pipeline,

the pipeline velocity, and how fast the opportunities are moving through that pipeline. Then we measure the direct marketing spend that we have and how that relates to new business," the finance leader explains. ∎

CFOTL: Tell us about a finance strategic moment.

Wookey: One that comes to mind began back in 2009, when I started at a company called Mindbody. We were a little bit bigger than Boulevard is now and we were a few rounds of investing ahead of where we are at Boulevard, but it was very clear that the business was growing extremely fast and that there was the potential that at some point in the future we might be able to become a public company. With this in mind, I knew that there were certain things that we needed to do at Mindbody to prepare for that moment—which didn't come until six years later. But in the time that I was heading finance there, what I tried to do was lay the foundation for what would be the ability to go public at some point in the future.

This really involved several things. One was to build out a more robust internal team in terms of accounting and finances and FP&A. Another was to create the ability to use tools that would be more supportive of a public company—for example, moving off of QuickBooks and onto NetSuite so that our reporting would be stronger. We also changed relationships in terms of our audit, banking, and legal. These were all things that I set in motion very early on in my career there. This eventually proved to be something that was important for the ability of the company to go public, which we did in 2015.

TO LISTEN

This was a moment when I looked at the finance operation, looked at what the state of it was at the time, and then thought about where it needed to be several years down the road. You have to start these processes in motion and not wait too long, or suddenly you're up against it in terms of timing. ∎

ENTERING THE AGE OF THE REAL-TIME CFO

GUEST CFO
MIKE ELLIS
Flywire

K nowing that Mike Ellis has been the CFO of several growth companies, we can't help but ask him about his tour of duty at the Massachusetts Port Authority, where the experienced finance executive served as controller from 2006 to 2009.

Although the Port Authority is not exactly the type of employer that you would expect to find on the resume of an accomplished "growth CFO," Ellis is more than happy to answer our question.

"The Port Authority was not tax-funded—it was a bona-fide business with multiple revenue streams generating profits," he explains, while characterizing the government agency as a $600 million business that contributes enormous value to the Commonwealth of Massachusetts.

"BEING ABLE TO ACHIEVE COLLABORATION AND INNOVATION AS A GROUP VERSUS HAVING TO JUST MAKE THE CALL MYSELF MADE ME A BETTER CFO."

"I had never worked for a not-for-profit from the inside, but what made me excited about the Port Authority was the sheer size of it," says Ellis, who during his tenure as controller would sign off on the accounting operations of three airports and a patchwork of revenue streams across Boston's sprawling seaport.

Looking back, Ellis says that up until the Port Authority, his senior finance leadership roles had permitted him to make decisions on his own,

whereas inside the Port Authority—as in any large enterprise businesses—decision-making had to be more collaborative.

"I had 40 people reporting to me at the Port Authority, and whether you are public or private or a not-for-profit business, decision-making has to be more collaborative," Ellis explains. "It was awkward at first, but in the end, being able to achieve collaboration and innovation as a group versus having to just make the call myself made me a better CFO," says Ellis, whose Port Authority career appears to have been well timed when you consider that it roughly coincided with the beginning of the CFO role's ongoing march toward requiring more overtly cross-functional leadership and regular collaboration with other functional groups and leaders. ■

CFOTL: Share with us some of the history behind the company's capital structure.

Ellis: I started with Flywire four years ago. We were basically a series C business at the time, basically a break-even business, so we really didn't need any additional capital. We have raised our series D, which came in approximately 18 months ago and was about a $100 million round. We've raised roughly $140 million for the business over the course of its nine-year history, and we still have plenty of it left. We've done a really good job of being efficient with our capital structure as well as making sure that the business model itself works appropriately and is efficient across all of its different tailored offerings to its customers. We're able to show that we're basically a moderately break-even business with respect to the business data analytics. We get real-time data on an hour-by-hour basis, essentially, so I'm able to understand our revenue and our transaction counts well by different verticals, by different geographic locations, by size, and by everything else across our different verticals. That's really robust, and there are no issues there. ■

SCAN ME

📱 TO LISTEN

ASSESSING THE HEALTH OF THE PORTFOLIO

GUEST CFO
ALAN GEORGE
Ojai Energetics

A mong the different experiences that Alan George credits with having prepared him for a CFO role, one office meeting looms large.

After he had spent days and nights preparing his first presentation for the president of a portfolio company, George recalls, the meeting came to an abrupt end when the executive reached across the table and shut George's laptop.

"WE WERE LITERALLY RIDING ON DELIVERY TRUCKS AND TALKING TO RETAILERS, AND HE TOOK ME THROUGH THROUGH THE ENTIRE LIFE CYCLE OF THE PRODUCT."

"Come with me!" was the curt command he recalls being issued as he followed the executive out of the office. Over the next few days, George says, he toured the company's manufacturing facility alongside the executive and went on visits to different suppliers.

"We were literally riding on delivery trucks and talking to retailers, and he took me through the entire life cycle of the product," says George, who credits the excursions with illuminating the realities of the business and delivering a lesson that to this day informs his decision-making.

Of course, the experience that truly sets George apart from those of most of our CFO guests is one that happened at midstream in his career, when—after having spent a number of years at JP Morgan as an investment analyst and ridden inside delivery trucks as a

SCAN ME

📱 TO LISTEN

private equity executive—he exited the business world and joined the U.S. military.

"I usually tell people that I took a five-year sabbatical," says George, who, after completing basic and airborne training, was selected as a Green Beret and assigned to a team within U.S. special forces with which he remained engaged for three years. "I was obviously older than most people, and I think that if I had waited three more months, I would have been over the age limit," explains George, who adds that a desire to serve in the military first took root while he was working at JP Morgan in New York in the months after 9/11. Six years later, his plans took flight. ■

Q&A

CFOTL: Tell us about your top-of-mind metrics and numbers...

George: The first thing that I look at is daily sales. I get a report that comes out in the middle of the night. I know what we did in sales the day before, and then I can drill down into it and say, OK, since I'm primarily a direct-to-consumer business, I want to see my traffic conversion and AOV. I want to see how we're doing relative to our forecast. I want to see how any specific programs are driving those key metrics. For us, specifically, traffic is a huge driver. We have really strong conversion and AOV. Traffic-driving awareness programs have a huge impact for our business. When we're looking at where we're spending marginal dollars, the ROI of driving traffic to our site today is really high, so the couple of betas that we've done to drive traffic have been really, really meaningful for us.

The other thing that I look at is repeat purchase rate. I think that this is an indicator of the health of your product portfolio and the quality of the products that you're delivering. I tell everybody that it's easy to get that first sale. It's really hard to get that second and almost impossible to get the third. So, how do we be the best at this? By getting our consumers to buy into what we're doing and continue to purchase. ■

USING OPENNESS TO ACHIEVE BUY-IN

GUEST CFO
ANUP SINGH
Illumio

A mong the more novel approaches that CFO Anup Singh has recently used to help advance a more open working environment at Illumio, of Sunnyvale, California, was the creation of a channel inside the instant messaging application Slack through which employees can access Illumio's finance leader by tagging their queries with an unassuming "#CFO ask me anything".

"They will ask me my views on things. This is about high employee engagement and being really accessible to the employees. I'm letting them know that they've got an avenue where we can be straightforward and very transparent with sharing information," says Singh, who joined Illumio in early 2019 after having served in the CFO role for several different companies, including Anaplan and Nimble Storage.

"AS A CFO, YOU ARE TRULY A CROSS-FUNCTIONAL EXECUTIVE. YOU'RE WEARING THE HAT OF A GM."

According to Singh, the CFO Slack channel extends his reach beyond his finance team members and helps him to communicate with
Illumio employees with whom he may not ordinarily engage.

Says Singh: "I can use the opportunity to explain the meaning of some of the financial analyses and metrics to a nonfinancial audience, and this is
information-sharing that is conversational."
At the same time, Singh's efforts to inject more openness into Illumio's finance function and the company at large have also involved more conventional methods.

Such is the case with "The Bottom Line," a label given to a number of somewhat impromptu meetings that Singh has held to better engage with Illumio employees.

"I do these a couple of times a quarter here at Illumio. It's off-the-cuff. I show up for an hour in the break room and employees can dial in from anywhere around the world and ask me questions," says Singh, who frequently uses the words "openness," "conversation," and "engagement" when describing the role of finance at Illumio.

"As a CFO, you are truly a cross-functional executive. You're wearing the hat of a GM. So this is about getting in there with sales and marketing and product people and sharing a very clear understanding of the value drivers and how your team helps the organization," he explains. ■

CFOTL: What are your priotiites as a finance leader over the next 12 months?

Singh: In looking ahead at Illumio, my big focus is on continuing to support our go-to-market expansion. Our company's growing quickly. We're expanding globally. This means recruiting in different geographies, expanding our offices, and so on. This is something that I and my team do a lot to support. In the past year, I would say that we've also worked hard to transform Illumio into a really data-driven environment as well as to emphasize the operational excellence of the company. The ongoing task is to continue to automate our metrics and automate our key processes. This obviously helps us to manage our growth efficiently. The last thing, which is very near and dear to my heart and a priority for me every year, is to continue the journey in building out a world-class team here at Illumio. This is an ongoing quest that we have. ■

SCAN ME

📱 TO LISTEN

FINANCE & THE BEAT OF THE DRUM

GUEST CFO
GUIDO TORRINI
Celonis

I t doesn't take long for CFO Guido Torrini of Celonis to draw our attention to the burden of the growing pools of data within organizations and the great irony that is afflicting many corporate finance departments today.

He's referring to the fact that while at no time have finance organizations had more data to help them better expose the opportunities that lie ahead, at no time has finance been at greater risk of losing the focus required to help their organizations benefit from the opportunities.

"You can't just throw new dashboards at people and make them awash in KPIs," observes Torrini, who believes that it's the responsibility of the CFO to first "distill the numbers" and then share them in a way that doesn't undermine the focus required for organizations to succeed.

"THIS IS ABOUT CRAFTING A MESSAGE AND DELIVERING IT OVER AND OVER AGAIN... AND THAT THERE'S A STRUCTURE AND CADENCE TO COMMUNICATING..."

"The ability to successfully execute is completely tied to focus," says Torrini, who underscores his point by recalling the "3 C's"—a favorite mantra of one of his early mentors, who implored his finance team to make every communication 'crisp, clear, and concise.'"

Beyond clarity, Torrini points out, messaging is about consistency and making certain that the organization as a whole is able to receive it.

"This is about crafting a message and delivering it over and over again, making sure that it goes across the organization and that there's a structure and cadence to communicating and reviewing it," notes Torrini, whose emphasis on "cadence" makes us think that he has perhaps added a fourth "C" to his mentor's mantra.

Says Torrini: "It's almost like a song that you find yourself repeating in your head without really understanding why." ∎

CFOTL: What are your priorities as a finance leader over the next 12 months?

Torrini: I like to describe the CFO as being kind of like the architect of the enterprise, in the sense of being someone who can actually design the machine and explain to people how the machine works and root every function in the organization in the revenue equation. This is how we make money. There are four or five important variables that matter at the company, and it's all about how everyone can align around how we move these variables up and down so that we grow and expand our business. I think that it's about not only providing the theoretical context for these, but also then leading people with the practical data and resolve and follow-through and monitoring that shows progress. Ultimately, you end up being not only the architect but also the drummer for the business—the one who sets the cadence and gives the rhythms on what's working, what's not working, and what we need to improve and on how we decide to allocate capital among the different initiatives, depending on what's yielding the best results.

I think that the CFO position is amazing because you have a unique vantage point in having the opportunity to run the data side of things as well as the finance function. The standards compliance and stewarding responsibilities are very enriching and something that I'm very excited about. Throughout my career, I've tried to progress and be ready to do more. You go from steward to operator to strategy, but I think that the bigger role that synthesizes it all is this idea of the architect and the drummer. ∎

SCAN ME
📱 TO LISTEN

RETHINKING SALES PRODUCTIVITY

GUEST CFO
CAROLYN KOEHN
Boomi

F or those finance chiefs who are apt to tweak their company's sales compensation plan, Boomi CFO Carolyn Koehn has some curt advice: Stop. Or at least make your tweaks sparingly.

"If you want to lose sales and have the sales team off doing exercises in game theory or whatever, just keep changing your comp plan," says Koehn, who served as vice president of finance, global sales compensation for the computer maker and storage company Dell until last year, when she stepped into the finance chief role at Boomi, a software-as-a-service (SaaS) company and Dell subsidiary.

Part of the temptation to "tweak" is due to the numerous inputs that feed into most sales comp plans, Koehn explains. The finance chief's admonition conjures a crowded control panel with dials that can be turned every which way.

"At Dell, we probably had 13 different inputs to calculate sales compensation and no salesperson cares where the tweaking error was made or who made it," says Koehn, who believes that sales productivity is at risk when inputs are being changed by different departments and functional groups within a company as well as different layers of management.

Koehn says that the sales team needs to get its marching orders from a single voice. "You have to have a team that owns sales compensation and knows how to reach into the organization to identify the problem, fix it, and be able to close that communication very quickly," explains Koehn. She adds that the key measures of success for sales compensation remain, first of all, the alignment between the goals of the business and the goals of the sales team. Disrupt the comp plan and Koehn warns that the sales team could be headed in a direction entirely unrelated to company goals. Koehn's second key measure of success

📱 TO LISTEN

for a comp plan is sales productivity—which brings us back to her admonition.

"I think that sales productivity is achieved by trying to keep the compensation plan as consistent as you can and, when you do have changes, try to keep them as simple as possible," observes Koehn, who says that while most comp calculations involve obvious numbers such as sales quotas and the dollar value of orders, the complexity quickly escalates when you factor in the overlapping sales rep assignments inside large customers and the bigger commissions offered by some products over others.

"DISRUPT THE COMP PLAN AND THE SALES TEAM COULD BE HEADED IN A DIRECTION ENTIRELY UNRELATED TO COMPANY GOALS."

"You can imagine that in a product portfolio as big as Dell's, there are a lot of opportunities to get it right, but there are also a lot of opportunities where errors can creep in," adds Koehn, who notes that calculating commissions for salespeople becomes even more challenging when human resources data is added to the mix.

"When was the salesperson's start date? When was their stop date? Did they get a pay raise? All of these elements usually aren't something that is necessarily top-of-mind, but get them wrong and you will certainly get commission payments incorrect," emphasizes Koehn.

Before accepting the CFO role at Boomi, Koehn says she had begun to look for future finance leadership roles that could provide broader management experience – the kind of experience that would someday make her an attractive candidate for outside board positions.

"Several folks approached me about the Boomi opportunity and I thought about what I could bring to the role and what it offered me in return," explains Koehn, who says from a personal development perspective Boomi ultimately transported her to a new land of opportunity. ∎

THE AWESOME POWER OF FP&A AN DECISION

GUEST CFO
JASON CHILD
Splunk

Inside the conference rooms of 21st-century businesses, few strategy debates have led to a decision as impactful as the one Amazon.com made in 2001.

In the wake of the dot-com crash, members of Amazon's fledgling financial planning and analysis, or FP&A, team became locked in a debate concerning customer shipping fees. Namely, whether the online retailer should do away with them completely.

"It's hard to imagine Amazon today without Prime or without free shipping," says Jason Child, a former Amazon FP&A executive whose team ultimately paved the way for Amazon's free shipping. Child remembers his involvement in Amazon's formative years and uses those experiences to impress on his current FP&A analysts the importance of the work. "That's the impact that we can have in FP&A,'" explains Child, who today is chief financial officer of Splunk, a fast-growing software developer that specializes in monitoring and analyzing machine-generated data.

Child first joined Amazon in 1999 as a corporate controller before migrating to the company's FP&A team. He would later serve in a number of finance leadership roles before leaving the company after a dozen years. Since his stint at Amazon, Child has occupied the CFO office at multiple companies, including Groupon—where less than a year after his arrival, the company would raise $700 million in an initial public offering, the second-biggest tech IPO in history at the time, behind Google's $1.7 billion IPO in 2004.

Amazon immediately springs to mind for Child when he lists career milestones. The online retailer grew into a colossus during his 12-years there, with annual revenue jumping from roughly $1 billion (1999) to $50 billion (2011) while its workforce exploded from about 5,000 employees to more than 100,000 within two years of his departure.

Child remembers that it was in 2001 when the shipping debate emerged. "My group was tasked with evaluating the impact of free shipping," explains Child. "What we found was that with free shipping, we were effectively giving only a 10% discount, but the resulting growth was two times higher than if we had given a 10% discount."

This realization led Amazon to explore how it could offer free shipping to its customers all the time. One obstacle was the "cannibalization" of existing revenue from customers who were not deterred by shipping fees and were willing to pay them. This snag led to a number of smaller meetings attended by Amazon's leader Jeff Bezos, in which Child introduced additional analysis on the cannibalization concern. Child recalls that Bezos was frustrated by the puzzle until another finance executive spoke up and suggested offering free shipping with a five day delay.

By comparing the "5-day delay" concept to "the Saturday night stay" tactic used by airlines to attract lower-fare consumers, Amazon's FP&A team began to achieve some traction. "People who want something in 2 days are going to pay for it, but everyone who wants free shipping will get their stuff in 5 days," says Child, who describes the 2001 shipping fees debate as foundational for the Amazon Prime program and Amazon's explosive growth. Child also remembers the period as providing the basis for his future CFO career. After little more than 2 years as a corporate controller, he joined the FP&A team and was assigned to the marketing department.

"Just being thrown into this environment where you had to learn and think about growth and how to build systems and processes that can grow 10 times bigger than they were at the time—this was a mind-set that I had not been exposed to before and that helped me to prepare for the next 20 years of my career," says Child, whose tenure inside the marketing department allowed him to collaborate with a number of Amazon's leaders, including Andy Jassy, the current CEO of Amazon Web Services. ∎

SCAN ME
📱 TO LISTEN

WHEN YOUR TWO WORLDS BECOME ONE

GUEST CFO
SHARI FREEDMAN
Room to Read

A t several points during the early years of her finance career, a tug-of-war was seemingly under way between the professional and personal worlds of Room to Read CFO Shari Freedman.

Back in the early 1990s, Freedman was running a homeless shelter in New York City while at the same time boarding flights for a string of international assignments on behalf of her then-employer, Pepsico. In 1995, when she relocated to San Francisco with apparel retailer Gap, she became involved with a workforce development organization dedicated to helping the unemployed and was soon asked to join its board and serve as president.

"I love being engaged in my communities," says Freedman, who left behind a decade of corporate career-building in large enterprise organizations at the turn of the new century to become a leader and board member of a mission-driven organization.

By 2014, having held multiple leadership roles in such entities, Freedman had decided that it was time to draw her professional and personal goals ever closer.

Thus she created a five-year plan for herself, a formula designed to help her make better decisions as she sought to steer herself to those opportunities capable of opening new doors.

"At that time, I specifically wrote that I wanted to work for an organization that was mission-centric and making a meaningful difference in the world, and I also wrote that I wanted to build a portfolio of girl students whose education we support and sponsor as a family," says Freedman, who likes to label herself as "a planner" and credits planning and goal-setting as central components of both her personal and professional worlds.

Says Freedman: "That goal-setting actually allowed me to narrow my decisions as to where my career would head and led me to Room to Read as their CFO". ■

CFOTL: What are your priorities as a finance leader over the next 12 months?

Freedman: Here at Room to Read, we've just launched our 2020–2025 strategic plan, of which one of the core parts is the continued build of our financial sustainability. I'm super excited and proud that we are launching a five-year, $10 million initiative—we're calling it a Future Fund—to which we're asking our donors to contribute. In addition to funding our day-to-day programs, we're looking to build out funds that will be unrestricted and allow us to get to six months' operating expense coverage, which is best-in-class. This would allow the organization to really build out its operational reserves to give us the wherewithal to weather ups and downs in the financial markets as well as to take some small risks with innovation to try some things out, test some things—to learn quickly and, if necessary, to fail quickly, as our board says—and to then adapt. Having those extra months of operating coverage will really make a difference for us.

My own organization has a leadership role in this, in partnership with the development team. We'll be talking to donors and working with all sorts of organizations to describe the need for having that kind of operating expense coverage to give us real sustainability for our future.

CFOTL: If you could go back in time, what would be the advice you would give yourself?

SCAN ME

▢ TO LISTEN

Freedman: I think the most under-invested part of the organizations are these smaller, under-financed organizations or highly leveraged organizations tends to be the accounting and finance teams. And so making sure that there's some good, solid investment behind those teams and that they really understand the underlying business precepts of what you're trying to do is so important. ■

FINDING YOUR GROOVE AGAIN AND AGAIN

GUEST CFO
LAURA ONOPCHENKO
NerdWallet

I t was still early in Laura Onopchenko's finance career when she removed "Chief Financial Officer" from the list of leadership roles that she aspired to someday hold.

"I very specifically made the call that I did not want to be a CFO," recalls Onopchenko, who says that at the time the decision seemed all the more contrarian, given her already-ingrained inclination to view the world through a financial lens.

"The reason that I was not attracted to the role was that I wildly underestimated how influential and how broad-based a good CFO can be and how unique the role is," says Onopchenko, who later "relisted" "CFO" as she began observing the evolutionary nature of the position and how finance leaders themselves were contributing to the role's development.

"IN THE TIME THAT I'VE BEEN CFO AT NERDWALLET, MY JOB HAS PROBABLY CHANGED THREE TIMES IN TERMS OF THE WORK I'M DOING."

"Part of our job as finance professionals is helping the role to evolve, and part of this is to continue to look for places where we can have an impact that might not be obvious," notes Onopchenko, who in 2017 entered the CFO office at NerdWallet, a personal finance company.

According to Onopchenko, the role of the CFO varies widely when you consider how companies demand new expertise and skillsets as businesses enter new stages of growth.

"In the time that I've been CFO at NerdWallet, my job has probably changed three times in terms of the work I'm doing," adds Onopchenko, who today dismisses her early impression of the role as being a one-size-fits-all scenario. Says Onopchenko: "There probably are about as many different CFO jobs today as there are CFOs." ■

CFOTL: What are your priorities as a finance leader over the next 12 months?

Onopchenko: We have a pretty rock-solid plan for the next 12 months. As we continue to experience really rapid growth at NerdWallet, we want to ensure that we have the infrastructure in place to support and enable this growth. One of the things that is really important for the finance and accounting team is to be just a few steps ahead of the rest of the organization. As an example, one of the things that we're going to be doing is working on building out our revenue operations team. The last thing that we want is for the company to be delivering revenue at a level that our team cannot support, such that we're not reporting at the rate that we are today or within the time frame that we are today or with the insights that we like to be able to provide to our partner teams now. We're really working on building that infrastructure in both finance and accounting, so we've got a plan for that.

The other thing is that we are always on the lookout for ways that our teams can help to contribute in new ways. So, while what I mentioned before is going to be the bulk of our work, I know that there are going to be a few new things that are going to pop onto our plate—places where we didn't realize that we had a role to play but where there is an opportunity for us to increase this business partnership to which we so aspire.

SCAN ME
TO LISTEN

We believe that, very simplistically, the combination of these two things—the more people who know about us and the more people we help to solve their financial challenges or answer their financial questions or help them answer their questions about their money—will in the long term position us really well for all of the exciting things that we believe are ahead. ■

APPLYING YOUR FRESH EYES TO THE ROLE

GUEST CFO
ANTHONY COLETTA
SAP North America

mong the job transitions that populated Anthony Coletta's early finance career, few likely paid more career dividends than the one that he made in 2006 when he leaped from Siemens to SAP.

While both positions were controller roles based in Paris, it's clear that Coletta quickly found the wind at his back at SAP, as a variety of international opportunities began to surface and propel him along an ever upward, worldwide course.

After filling a number of senior controllership roles inside SAP's North American region, Coletta held a series of finance leadership posts in Latin America and the Caribbean before being named CFO of Mexico and Central America, after which he then stepped into the CFO office of SAP North America in 2018. ◼

CFOTL: When it comes to finance strategic moments of insight, what would you share with us?

Coletta: The most recent strategic moment that sticks with me goes back two years to when I moved to our North America organization as CFO. We were on the battlefield of innovation and the cloud business, and we were carrying a big share of the company's business, with high expectations on the streets already. We had a business that had been a bit bumpy in the beginning of the year, but we had a solid team that was always seeking to improve itself. To me, it was, Okay, what do I bring to the table and how do I change the dynamic here? The good news was that we had a lot to work with, but the bad news was that when you are public and in a very exposed environment, you never have as much time as you'd like. It's very important not only to deliver quickly, but also to change or invert some trends.

I really make sure that I bring value to the business. My team and I give advice and make fact-based decisions that really form a success plan for the remainder of the year at any given time. The strategic moment for me came at the end of the year. We had a very sound acceleration and great financial results, and the team got recognized as Finance Region of the Year. We had gotten employee engagement going up, as well as leadership trust. Service attitudes with regard to the business were way above the benchmarks, and all of this was performed with quality, so we had gained in predictability, efficiency, energy, and credibility. Obviously, the credit goes to the team all together, and this takes an entire leadership team really rising to the occasion. But it's quite powerful to see how dynamics can change and how you can sustain success when you focus on the right things.

"IT'S QUITE POWERFUL TO SEE HOW DYNAMICS CAN CHANGE AND HOW YOU CAN SUSTAIN SUCCESS WHEN YOU FOCUS ON THE RIGHT THINGS."

This strategic moment for me was then when I entered that office and got so much responsibility put in front of me. There were a lot of areas to improve—I won't say "fix"—but to improve. At the same time, we had a very high run rate, and some areas were doing fairly well. We had a business environment that was quite steady, a big customer base, and so on. So, how do you really drive change in a short period of time, which in this case was the seven months left in the year to make an impact and turn the ship, so to speak? We have been riding this wave ever since. We have a lot of positive momentum across the board on the business front and also in finance, and I think that inverting some of the trends at the right time was critical. ◼

FORTIFYING YOUR FP&A FOOTING

GUEST CFO
ROBERT RICHARDS
Centauri

 Recalling a meeting that took place years ago at an industry conference, CFO Robert Richards remembers that the East Coast sales executive's face suddenly dropped.

At the time, Richards was more or less his company's de facto CFO after the company's finance leader had departed in the wake of the firm defaulting on certain loans. Being only in his mid-20s and with his company's reputation preceding him, Richards found it hard to generate favorable first impressions—a fact particularly true with the struggling company's suppliers.

Lobbying the vendors for better credit terms was a top priority for Richards, leading him to attend a number of industry conferences where he sought to nurture credit relationships through in-person meetings.

"WE WENT FROM A DOUBLE-DIGIT MARGIN LOSS IN ONE YEAR TO A DOUBLE-DIGIT MARGIN PROFIT THE NEXT."

The East Coast sales executive could not conceal his dismay when Richards introduced himself, but the meeting yielded a fruitful outcome.

"I was able to sell them on the opportunity and supporting us and the exciting growth that we might achieve together," explains Richards, who credits the newly modified credit terms with having helped to turn around the company.

Says Richards: "We went from a double-digit margin loss in one year to a double-digit margin profit the next, with a new credit facility negotiated."

Asked to identify experiences that prepared him for a CFO leadership role, Richards says that the memory of the executive's face dropping has never faded and always returns him to the circumstances and challenges of that place in time.
"That year or two was probably the most important period in my career as far as being formative goes and learning about what's required to work through a crisis," he explains. ∎

CFOTL: Tell us about this business. What does it do and what are its offerings?

Richards: Centauri is a government services business. We've been growing at about 20% a year, on an organic-only basis, for the past four or five years. We just reached just under $500 million in revenue in 2019, and I'm looking to continue growing in the 20% to 30% range in 2020. We're really focused on space and missile defense and where those domains intersect and create sort of an ecosystem in the defense world. We focus on employing what we believe really is our strength, which is the top technical and specialized talent needed to support the missions of our customers. What makes us different from other government services providers is our focus on the people. I think that a lot of government services companies see the billable staff as not really employees of the company but just products that are being sold. When one contract goes away, so do their products, and when you get a new contract, you go hire new people.

We really focus on our technical talent as part of the company. They're not tied to a specific contract or project, but we will develop their career, invest in them from a training and professional development perspective, and move them between projects so that they get enhanced skills that allow them to move up in their career. ∎

SCAN ME
▢ TO LISTEN

ENTERING WITH AN APPETITE FOR CHANGE

GUEST CFO
TOD NESTOR
Energy Focus

T od Nestor remembers his first performance review like it was yesterday.

Sitting across from his manager inside the offices of Pepsico's Purchase, New York, headquarters, Nestor recalls receiving a pat on the back before the manager's feedback began to sting.

"It seemed like there were two minutes of 'Here's what you're doing well' and two hours of 'Here's where you have to do better.' I walked out of there pretty angry and frustrated," explains Nestor, who says that he later circled Pepsico's spacious campus twice on a long midday walk.

"WHEN I ACCEPTED THE FACT THAT FEEDBACK ABOUT PERFORMANCE WAS SOMETHING THAT COULD MAKE ME BETTER—AND NOT JUST CRITICISM—MY LIFE CHANGED."

"By the time I began my second loop, I had told myself that '90 percent of what that individual just told me was correct,'" says Nestor, who subsequently began viewing the manager's feedback not only as being largely accurate but also as a valuable commodity.

"When I accepted the fact that feedback about performance was something that could make me better—and not just criticism—my life changed," he acknowledges.

SCAN ME

📱 TO LISTEN

Going forward, Nestor says that he looked for feedback inside every corporate corridor.

"People got sick of me trying to pull the stuff out of them," says Nestor, who believes that while he did not always respond to feedback, he did always listen to it and carefully consider whether he should respond. ■

CFOTL: Tell us about this company. What does it do, and what are its offerings today?

Nestor: Energy Focus is an LED lighting and controls company. LED lighting is like comparing a smartphone to a rotary phone. LED lights are actually extremely high-tech—it's almost like having a laptop inside the light. If you were to take one apart, you would be amazed at how many computer components and wafers and chips are in there. These lights are not a commodity. They are very differentiated. Unfortunately, the industry historically has sold them very much like a commodity, through the same channels as fluorescent and incandescent lights. Energy Focus does not. One thing that sets us apart is that we use a direct sales model, which does give us, we think, a competitive advantage.

We will soon be launching a new product that has dimmable and tunable LED lighting. It allows you to leverage your existing wiring without having to use Bluetooth or wifi or do a big rewiring in a facility. This is coming out in the market soon, and we think that it will be revolutionary. The people who have seen the demos have been very excited about it. This type of approach is what sets us apart.

I think that we're a very unique company that is positioned very well in an industry that's going to be growing extraordinarily rapidly over the next 10 years. The key to success is growth, profitable growth, and we will do that. I really want to return Energy Focus to cash flow break-even—this is a very important goal for the next 12 months. We will be getting this new product launched successfully, and of course I'm always focused on generating shareholder returns. ■

KEEPING AN EYE ON YOUR KPIS

GUEST CFO
OMAR CHOUCAIR
Trintech

 long his path to the CFO office at technology firm Trintech, Omar Choucair's segue from radio to high tech was among his most consequential career transitions.

"There were not a lot of radio companies based in Dallas, Texas, at the time, and there was this young but growing tech company. While it was a calculated risk on my part, I liked the people, and the executives were hard-charging, which I also liked," says Choucair, when asked to recall some of the decision-making behind his leap to the high-tech realm.

"THE DIFFICULT PART LIES IN ORGANIZING THE FP&A TEAM... INTO A FORM THAT PEOPLE CAN REALLY LOOK TO AND USE TO MAKE DECISIONS."

Today, as Trintech's finance leader, Choucair has a list of CFO priorities that includes making performance measures more accessible across the organization.

When it comes to Trintech's approach to FP&A, Choucair is typically analytical: "I think that the bones are there and the data are there, but the difficult part lies in organizing the FP&A team around the question of how we get this put together into a form that people can really look at and use to make decisions."

Choucair says that he wants people to second-guess the factors currently driving performance and that they should be routinely asking the question, "Why did this happen

last week or last month versus three months ago?"

One recent development that is helping to energize performance measurement at Trintech as well as across the Software-as-a-Service (SaaS) realm is the broadening publication of KPIs.

"Today, versus a couple of years ago, we now have many of these public companies publishing their KPIs through their Investor Day presentation decks or their 10-K and 10-Q financial filing disclosures. So there's a lot of information that we can now mine in order to track how we're doing when compared to everybody else," explains Choucair. ∎

CFOTL: Tell us about your experiences inside the high tech industry?

Choucair: Trintech is my third technology company as CFO. Immediately before this, I was with a software company that was another private equity–backed firm that sold digital advertising on a subscription basis. We had a platform that was a B2B play and very competitive with a lot of the other technology companies that were selling into B2B with marketers all across the U.S. Before that, my first CFO opportunity was with a technology software company that distributed TV commercials and other short-term content on behalf of advertisers and marketers to television stations and cable outlets. So, I've been in an interesting space in that I've been in three different technology companies and the last two were SaaS. The first one was software, but it was sold by the drink.

I think that what's interesting about this business is that there's a significant opportunity on the large enterprise side. The office of the CFO has changed tremendously in the sense that there are so many different applications that you can bring to automate a lot of the functions, whether it's your financial planning, your tax compliance, and so forth. It could be your payroll; it could be your travel; it could be your HR. ∎

SCAN ME

📱 TO LISTEN

A TASTE FOR OPPORTUNITY

GUEST CFO
ANKUR AGRAWAL
Cooks Venture

A s the newly appointed CFO of agtech start-up Cooks Venture, Ankur Agrawal lists one of his favorite duties as designing menus. Of course, we are referring to the menu of performance measurements featured on the poultry company's maturing business dashboard.

"One of the beauties that comes with joining a new company is that you get to build from scratch," explains Agrawal, who says that he's relied on some of his earlier experiences using dashboards at Pepsico and Blue Apron to help Cooks Venture to build a better one.

According to Agrawal, a successful dashboard begins with understanding what measurements are needed inside a company's different business functions. At Blue Apron, Agrawal says, the firm's finance leader improved the company's dashboard design by first asking functional leaders across the company, "What are the two or three measurements that you are looking at?"

"Once he got that list from everyone, he said, 'All right, now let's create our dashboard.' I've tried to take a similar approach in which we talk to people and try to understand what they need to see," explains Agrawal, whose tour of duty at Blue Apron offered far more than lessons in dashboard design.

As a finance director for the innovative meal-kit company, Agrawal worked closely with Blue Apron's cofounder and COO, Matt Wadiak, who left the company in 2017 to establish Cooks Venture.

Says Agrawal: "We had worked closely for four years. We had a great partnership and complemented each other very well. We had been talking for a while, so when he started this company, essentially it became the right time for the business and for me because I had been looking for the right opportunity." ∎

TO LISTEN

Q&A

CFOTL: Tells about your priorities when you first stepped into the CFO role at Cooks Venture?

Agrawal: Big company or small company, your job in the very beginning is just to listen. There's a reason why things may be done a certain way, so I don't believe in going in and reorganizing or things like that. I really want to listen first to understand what's working, what's not working, what our team's skill sets are, what the areas to develop are. Then, after that, I'll start looking into, "Hey, do we need to operate differently? Do we need to enhance our team in any way?" We haven't gotten to that point yet, and currently I'm just continuing to learn the business. I've learned the team, but in the future, I think that as we grow and have to become bigger, such inquiries will definitely become an important area.

"WE FIND CREATIVE SOLUTIONS TO MAKE THINGS WORK, WHETHER IT'S A NEW INGREDIENT, A NEW PRODUCT, A NEW PROCESS."

You want to focus on building the finance culture. People can have varying degrees of what finance means to them, but for me, finance is an enabler for growth. We find creative solutions to make things work, whether it's a new ingredient, a new product, a new process. So, I really try to instill that culture into every company I've joined. Hey, we are partners. Our job really is to make sure that everyone else at the company is successful, and that's when we've done our job well. I have tried to make sure that the culture is very clear from the very beginning and that we're not a function that's there to say "No!" ∎

KEEPING AN EYE ON YOUR KPIS

GUEST CFO
BILL KOEFOED
OneStream Software

When asked whether a new sales enablement hire would be a "direct report," Bill Koefoed, CFO of OneStream Software, replied: "Organization matters only when your processes and relationships don't."

It's an observation not shared widely perhaps among newbie CFOs, who upon their arrival are known to rely more on organizational reporting lines than relationship potential to assert their influence.

Nevertheless, four months and one pandemic into his latest CFO tour of duty, Koefoed has his relationship-building skills in high gear as he works alongside OneStream's sales leaders to better identify those factors contributing to sales productivity.

According to Koefoed, the challenge is not just about sales productivity, though, but also about how to make the team productive more quickly. Hence OneStream's new sales enablement hire.

Says Koefoed: "People don't have to sit in finance to be effective, and having great partners and relationships in other areas of the business is just a great way to run the business."

In addition to sales, Koefoed's relationship-building skills also appear to be focused on OneStream's customers. How long a customer has been in the pipeline frequently correlates to deal size, says Koefoed, who concedes, "Obviously, big deals take longer."

Still, Koefoed says that his focus these days is more on something that he refers to as "customer familiarity"—and here, too, he's looking for ways to accelerate OneStream's upward climb on his customer awareness meter.

"The more familiar somebody is with your company, the better able they are to make key decisions," adds Koefoed, who note that in the case of OneStream, "key decisions" are what trigger the movement of customers to OneStream's software offerings and away from software provided by larger, more established rivals. ■

CFOTL: Having worked in the Bay area for most of your career, tell us about your arrival at OneStream and the opportunity that brought you to Michigan?

Koefoed: After I got a call from a recruiter to come and see this company, the more that I pulled the covers back, the more that I liked about it. It's really a company that was born out of a lot of folks who had deep experience with Hyperion, which, as as many know, was really the standard for consolidation and reporting and planning and analysis for the biggest companies in the world for a long time. It was acquired by a large software company in the Bay area, and now we've really built a modern, cloud-based, next-generation product that allows the finance organization to do all of those finance functions in a really modern and cloud-based way.

We're based in Rochester, Michigan, which is not the Bay area but does have good universities and has attracted quite a talented team to build upon. We don't actually have the same competitive dynamics that the Bay area has, which is a really big advantage for us. We did over $130 million in 2019 and grew by over 50%. We have aspirations to continue to grow the business at a pretty rapid pace.

When I look at the next year, it's overwhelming but really exciting. It's all about having a great team, building a great team, and having fun in your job every day, which is one of the things that I would recommend for everybody. It's easy to say, but life's too short: Have fun in your job. If you're not having fun, then reevaluate the job that you're doing or go get a new one. I really think that the difference between success and failure in life depends on whether you're having fun. ■

SCAN ME

📱 TO LISTEN

FINTECH GOES BEYOND THE PAYCHECK

GUEST CFO
BRIAN WHALEN
Branch

B ack in 2008, when auction giant eBay acquired Bill Me Later (BML), a Maryland-based payment credit company, Brian Whalen and his BML colleagues breathed a sigh of relief.

"We had just enough liquidity and options to give us the runway to sell to eBay and PayPal, so—from a learning perspective—it was really about asking the questions 'How do you keep those options open?' and 'How do you keep your liquidity choices available to you so that you can capture the moment?'" says Whalen.

Having served in a number business development roles at BML, he recalls as if it were yesterday the sudden wallop that the credit crisis delivered: "It hit us like a sledgehammer, so we made the decision to tighten credit and sacrifice some growth for the quality of our assets."

"PEOPLE WILL JOKE AND SAY, 'IT'S BETTER TO BE LUCKY THAN GOOD,' BUT TO A CERTAIN EXTENT, WE MADE OUR OWN LUCK BY BEING PREPARED."

In addition to preserving cash, BML would raise $100 million from Amazon and T. Rowe Price, while having discussions with a string of potential suitors. Ultimately, in October 2008, eBay acquired the firm for $820 million in cash and approximately $125 million in stock.

"People will joke and say, 'It's better to be lucky than good,' but to a certain extent, we made

our own luck by being prepared," explains Whalen, who relocated to California following the acquisition of BML to serve in a number of business development and finance roles at PayPal headquarters, including CFO of PayPal's global credit group. Eventually, he stepped back onto a more entrepreneurial FinTech path that has led him to the CFO office at Branch, a start-up specializing in what are widely labeled as "financial wellness" offerings for companies and their employees. ∎

CFOTL: Tell us about this company and what sets it apart from its competitors today?

Whalen: Branch really moved from being a SaaS business into having sort of this FinTech banking-like business model. I had been doing FinTech for 20 years, probably before it was even called FinTech. Having seen all of the range of possible outcomes from a FinTech business and a great exit to PayPal and having sold a couple of companies at a much lower valuation to other people, for me this was all about leveraging my understanding of how to build out unit economics and really invest in the business. How do we manage liquidity, debt, and equity so that we can have the best runway possible? This is really where the overlap between me and what Branch needed was critical.

As the first CFO, I am building out the financial systems and controls, laying the common ground for future financial employees, and instituting an analytical framework and processes so that we can make sound decisions on growth. We need to make sure that we're investing where we need to. We need to develop and manage our liquidity strategy that I referred to earlier to ensure that we have options available to us so that if we go and find a large employer that we want to sign, we have the liquidity to grow with these big opportunities. These are really all elements of the same challenge, which is just to establish the proper tools so that Branch can grow effectively and profitably. ∎

SCAN ME

📱 TO LISTEN

BUILDER, FIXER, FINANCE CHIEF

GUEST CFO
BOB FELLER
Workforce Software

L ast November, CFO Bob Feller achieved a career milestone of sorts when he celebrated his fifth anniversary as Workforce Software's finance leader.

"Prior to this, the longest that I have ever stayed anywhere has been four years," explains Feller, who says that the cadence of his CFO career transitions is normally in step with those of other tech sector CFOs, who are known to job-hop every three to four years.

Still, Feller mentions his recent anniversary to draw our attention to his resolve to help build Workforce into a formidable SaaS challenger inside the realm of workforce management software.

"WITH EVERY DEAL THAT WE CLOSE, WE PRETTY MUCH TAKE MARKET SHARE FROM KRONOS," SAYS FELLER.

"It reminds me of when I started at Salesforce and we were up against Siebel—which was then acquired by Oracle—and everyone thought that we didn't have a chance," says Feller, who held controller and VP of finance roles during a four-year stint at Salesforce. Feller says that Salesforce's singular focus as a SaaS company allowed it to overstep its merged rivals, who—while many times the size of Salesforce—failed to exploit all of the maturing advantages of the SaaS model.

Feller believes that this rivalry was similar to one that Workforce has today with HR software behemoth Kronos, of Lowell, Massachusetts.

"With every deal that we close, we pretty much take market share from Kronos," says Feller, while naming the widely known rival that is roughly 15 times the size of Workforce.

Says Feller: "We like to say that we're 'Zeus to Kronos'—and if you don't know your Greek mythology, just search 'Zeus, son of Kronos' and you will discover just what Zeus ended up doing to Kronos." Needless to say, there's a reason that Zeus, and not his father, was known as ruler of the gods. ■

CFOTL: Tell us about your arrival at Workforce and what this career chapter means for you?

Feller: How has my career evolved? I tend to be a builder and a fixer. I come into situations when some kind of a transformational event either has happened or is about to happen. This obviously goes back to Salesforce, where I had to build a team as we were building the company and prepping for an IPO, and has continued on to Workforce, where the company was founder-led for a number of years. You know, the founder did a great job in building the company, but it was really his first job out of business school. His first job out of business school was being our CEO. This happens all the time. The company did a lot of things well, but on the administration side, there was a lot of work to be done.

When we were acquired by Insight Venture Partners in 2014, I was the first hire that they made. They were looking for an experienced SaaS CFO who really knew how to put together not just a team but also the appropriate SaaS company metrics—the KPIs—and who knew how to work with a private equity firm and build a team to support that. Yes, this took time, but this is part of what I do to transform an organization. ■

SCAN ME
📱 TO LISTEN

THE ART OF FIXING WHAT'S BROKEN

GUEST CFO
TERRY SCHMID
Topia

Purchasing bananas and moving them through a warehouse in less than 24 hours is perhaps not a professional experience widely shared by today's finance leaders. Still, as Topia CFO Terry Schmid tells it, mastering banana logistics may just be a worthy prerequisite for many of today's CFO roles.

"It taught me to think about the process that you go through to understand how things flow, how things actually work, and how you can improve things," says Schmid, who first entered the professional world as a software coder specializing in COBOL—a language that landed him a consulting engagement with Safeway, Inc., in the 1990s, where he spent months alongside a team of Safeway buyers building a new logistics and warehousing system.

"AUTOMATION HAS A TENDENCY TO UNNERVE PEOPLE. IT WAS MY JOB TO CONVINCE THESE GUYS THAT USING THE SYSTEM WAS GOING TO BE BENEFICIAL TO THEM AND MAKE THEIR JOB BETTER."

"Being responsible for the produce piece, I had to learn how they buy produce and move it through the warehouse, after which we wrote a system to automate the process to a large degree—particularly the buying part," explains Schmid, who recalls the Safeway team as being at first somewhat doubtful about the new system.

"Automation has a tendency to unnerve people. It was my job to convince these guys that using the system was going to be beneficial to them and make their job better. It wasn't going to replace them. It was just going to make their job simpler," he recalls.

Schmid doesn't hesitate to draw a line from his COBOL coding days straight to the CFO office. "The opportunity that I got out of that was a solid understanding of how businesses work, how information flows, and how important it is that information is timely and accurate," notes Schmid, who characterizes the CFO role as one dedicated to helping organizations fix broken processes or adopt new ones in order to clear the path for growth. This is a role widely coveted inside the tech sector, but few CFOs have been as frequently recruited as Schmid, who has to date served as CFO in more than a half-dozen early-stage companies.

Twelve months into his latest CFO role, at Topia, Schmid is back to fixing processes and studying workflows and purchase patterns just as he did in the 1990s. In one way or another, it seems that he's been moving bananas ever since. ∎

SCAN ME

📱 TO LISTEN

CFOTL: Having served as a CFO of multiple early-stage companies, what's different about Topia? What sets this opportunity and the challenges it faces apart?

Schmid: Every job and every company is different and has its own challenges. A lot of it is the same on a fundamental level with regard to what it is that you need to get done every day, but the challenges of a company and where it's at at any given point in time are always different. Topia is a great company in a great space at a great time, but we're also working through some operational challenges that have built up over the past few years. We've effectively had to reboot the company, and more than 50% of it has become new from a personnel perspective, as we've had to change over and bring people in who can help us to scale the business. Can we grow this business? ∎

WHY CFOS MUST ASK DIFFICULT QUESTIONS

GUEST CFO
ANDREW CASEY
WalkMe

Years from now, when Andrew Casey reflects back on his CFO career and seeks to make sense of its various chapters, he may want to title the mythical volume Timing Is Everything. Certainly, few expressions might better summarize the career path of a finance executive who for years diligently checked off each CFO prerequisite only to arrive in the CFO office in March 2020—the very month when industry faced the seismic consequences of COVID-19.

"YOU LEARN FROM THE GOOD TIMES AND THE DOWN TIMES, BUT WHEN FINANCE IS MOST IMPORTANT TO AN ORGANIZATION IS THE DOWN TIMES."

No matter what lies ahead for Casey—or how he chooses to label his arrival in the C-suite at SaaS digital adoption enabler WalkMe—there's little doubt that COVID-19 and industry's response to it will become a defining chapter of his finance career.

Says Casey: "You learn from the good times and the down times, but when finance is most important to an organization is the down times because finance is the unbiased party in the room with respect to employee priorities as well as overall priorities."

Turn back the clock to 2019, when Dan Adika, CEO of WalkMe, was meeting with Casey to make the case for the widening appeal of WalkMe's digital offerings. "About halfway through the meeting, I said, 'This is one of the strangest interviews I've ever had,' and he asked, 'Why is that?' I said, 'It feels like you're just pitching me on the company.' He stopped midstream and looked me in the eye and said, 'Well, you know, we're already convinced about you. We're just trying to sell WalkMe to you.' At that moment, I knew that I could ask any question, and I knew that my rapport with Dan was going to be strong," recalls Casey, who at the time was a senior vice president of finance for cloud computing giant ServiceNow. "At that moment," there was little question that for Casey, timing was everything. ∎

CFOTL: Tell us about your arrival at WalkMe and how you've begun to prioritize the work that lies ahead?

Casey: One of the first things that I've done is to let people know who I am—that I have a family, that I have aspirations for myself and for the company, and that these things are very much interlocked. I want them to understand that I am not here to just come in and put my stamp on things—that I am here to really try to help architect the right organization with business processes that support our overall company objectives. The first priority for me is building the foundation for a world-class finance group. This starts with understanding the needs of the business and then what functions and processes we need to build in place. I've seen what it looks like to be in a world-class execution company. I would say that we don't have this yet, but we're going to build it.

One of my first steps is to build some core processes and build out the organization. This means having a forecasting process. We're talking about having a pricing strategy and having some discipline and cadence with our sales team on their selling process and partnering with the businesses to do this. This is about partnering with our sales leader and partnering with our services leader to make sure that we're ready to have an execution machine in place so that when the opportunities are there, we can take advantage of them with my team here for support. ∎

📱 TO LISTEN

THE INCENTIVE TO WIDEN YOUR LENS

GUEST CFO
SAMEER BHARGAVA
Clark Construction Group

Having built a successful career in private equity with 13 of those years with the formidable and clandestine Carlyle Group, Sameer Bhargava was probably not the most likely candidate to fill a CFO position at Clark Construction Group of Bethesda, Maryland.

The two businesses belonged to strikingly different worlds. Whereas Carlyle's populated its world with leading edge investment vehicles and innovative global assets, Clark populated its with signature skyscrapers and civic projects that are today credited with transforming public space.

Still, both businesses – headquartered in the greater Washington, DC area – share what arguably remains industry's greatest hiring determinant – a common geography.

For its part, Clark Construction's resume is filled with "home town"projects of stature including The Wharf – a pedestrian- oriented DC waterfront community and the National Museum of African American History and Culture.

"IN MEDICINE AND OTHER INDUSTRIES, YOU GET BETTER AND SMARTER THE MORE SPECIALIZED YOU BECOME. WHEREAS IN BUSINESS IT'S QUITE THE OPPOSITE."

"Every block that you drive by, Clark is building something incredibly impressive,"

remarks Bhargava, who quickly emphasizes Clark's national footprint by mentioning other Clark credits including San Francisco's Salesforce Tower and San Antonio's Frost Tower.

While Bhargava's enthusiasm for Clark's work is evident, he makes clear his move to Clark was driven by more than geography and the firm's A-list menu of cityscape projects.

"In medicine and other industries, you get better and smarter the more specialized you become. Whereas in business it's quite the opposite," says Bhargava, who encourages others to "take the risk to be uncomfortable" and "do things differently." ■

Q&A

CFOTL: Tell us about Clark – what is it known for? What types of projects has it been involved with?

Bhargava: Clark is a 114-year-old company with $5 billion in revenue nationwide. We are one of the biggest firms, we are commercial- and civil-focused, and we build across the country. I think that we are the largest U.S. privately held construction company out there. We have hundreds of projects going on at any given time across the country, in all different sectors of public and private work. We employ about 4,000 people around the country, plus many subcontractors and other people at our job sites.

Our projects range from the Chase Center and Salesforce Tower in San Francisco to a new terminal at the Kansas City International Airport to the National Museum of African-American History and Culture in Washington, D.C. We've done a lot of hospitals, including one at Fort Bliss, Texas. There's the the Frost Tower in San Antonio, the National Air and Space Museum in Washington, and McCormick Place in Chicago. We also have civil projects like roads, bridges, and tunnels going on across much of America.

There's always something big and prominent and complex that we're working on. ■

SCAN ME

📱 TO LISTEN

ENERGIZING YOUR CUSTOMER BORDERS

GUEST CFO
JIM EMERICH
Narvar

F or many future finance leaders, the year 2020 is destined to provide the dark moments of doubt that sweeten the upsides to be savored in years to come.

Certainly, few business lessons are more widely cherished than those related to challenging economic times—and few are summoned more by finance leaders when it comes to explaining their business-building philosophies.

Such is the case with Narvar CFO Jim Emerich, who in recounting the experiences that have prepared him for a finance leadership role always singles out the year 2001, when the September 11 terrorist attacks disrupted an economy still reeling from the burst of the dotcom bubble.

"WHAT SAVED US WAS THE KNOWLEDGE THAT EVENTUALLY PEOPLE REALIZED THAT THE WORLD HADN'T ENDED."

That May, Emerich stepped into a controller position at Salesforce, the pioneering SaaS developer that had only recently entered the ranks of midsize companies.

"We were burning cash throughout that year, and we were getting pretty close to the end. What saved us was the knowledge that eventually people realized that the world hadn't ended," recalls Emerich, who confidently and swiftly draws a line from his early Salesforce days to his arrival at Narvar earlier this year. As at Salesforce, Emerich is now tasked with building the financial infrastructure of a SaaS developer in the midst of economic uncertainty. But now is a time well suited to experienced leaders accustomed to quelling doubts and exposing the path to the future. ■

CFOTL: Please share some thoughts on COVID 19's impact on the business and what steps you may be taking to manage the business in this challenging environment?

Emerich: This is a humanitarian challenge that we're dealing with here. It's completely global in that everybody's impacted by this. Having said this, I think that there are definitely some things that we can do internally. We're now looking at our costs, and we're thinking about things that we can trim back. But we also know that there are opportunities out there for partnering with our customers to help to make them successful throughout all this. There are opportunities for us because of what we do. We're helping traditional retailers and businesses that are typically doing digital themselves or they're heavily into stores and they need a digital presence right now. They need an e-commerce component, so there's interesting opportunity here for us.

When I reflect back on Salesforce, for instance, I think, "Why did we succeed?" It wasn't that much fun when I got there, to be frank about it. I was working probably 16-hour days. It was 2001. I was happy to have a job because the market had imploded and Salesforce was one of the few tech companies that was still around that was of some size. But we were burning cash throughout that year, and we were getting pretty close to the end. What saved us was the knowledge that eventually people realized that the world hadn't ended. There was a lot of tragedy going in the world, and it was right after 9/11 on top of that, but business still needed to function like the world hadn't ended. ■

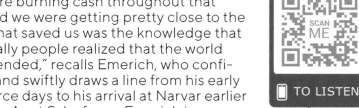

SCAN ME

📱 TO LISTEN

THE ART & SCIENCE OF RAISING FUNDS

GUEST CFO
CHRIS MAUSLER
PeerNova

When it comes to raising money from the investor community, finance executives often find themselves standing in line for job assignments that promise to make them active participants in the process.

Such roles allow aspiring finance leaders to check off one of the more essential items on the demanding list of prerequisites required of high-growth-. firm CFOs.

For those executives who have climbed the accounting career ladder or toiled for years in an FP&A cubicle, the "money box" is often one of the last ones to get checked off.

Such was the case for finance leader Chris Mausler, who after a decade of devouring high-calorie FP&A assignments at IBM Corp. exited the computer giant to join a string of Silicon Valley firms.

"I'M CERTAIN THAT THERE ARE COMPANIES OUT THERE THAT MAKE THEIR FIRST PITCH AND GET FUNDED WITH A TERM SHEET, BUT THIS IS NOT THE NORM."

Removed from IBM's sprawling organization, Mausler found himself in closer proximity to the action. Nevertheless, it would take years for the seasoned FP&A executive to land a role that allowed him to check that box and ultimately raise money for a variety of different firms.

"Even though my assignments had touched on treasury-type operations in an indi-

rect way, I myself had actually never directly raised money before," says Mausler, who last fall helped to raise $31 million in funding for San Jose, California's PeerNova, the data governance company that he joined as CFO back in 2014.

"I'm certain that there are companies out there that make their first pitch and get funded with a term sheet, but this is not the norm," says Mausler, who notes that most companies can expect to receive only a handful of term sheets from roughly 100 pitches.

"It's a little bit of an art, a little bit of a science for anyone going through it," he adds. ∎

Q&A

CFOTL: What are your priorities as a finance leader in this new economic environment?

Mausler: As I'm sitting here at home under a shelter-in-place order, my first priority clearly is to manage our company over the next couple of months to make sure that we don't lose any efficiency and effectiveness in meeting our short-term goals, and this is certainly a new challenge through these times. Other than that, the challenges that I have remain much the same at PeerNova. We raised a good financing last fall. We announced a $31 million round that's going to take us for a while. We have goals and milestones for getting us through a large kind of growth round in the future. We've got to make sure that we get there, so it's making sure that we're hitting the near-term milestones and tweaking our strategy to hit the next ones.

Here at PeerNova we had good data, so it was just a question of organizing it into one place so that we could manage the business. It's been very much of a journey for us as we've raised rounds to build out this platform and worked with early customers on projects to grow our business. The most critical thing at PeerNova has been to raise the right amount of capital to help to get us to the next set of milestones and to make the right set of investments to get to these milestones so that we can continue to grow the company and keep this kind of growth pattern going. ∎

SCAN ME

📱 TO LISTEN

THE FLIGHT TO DIGITAL

GUEST CFO
VIRPY RICHTER
Awin Global

I t was supposed to be the type of introduction that would help to break the ice between a new business leader and her direct reports. However, the words spoken by the managing director (MD) became frozen in time.

Or at least in the memory of Virpy Richter, who at the age of 27 had only recently relocated from Germany after having accepted a promotion to oversee the finances of her company's Dutch operating unit.

"This is the German girl from our central unit. Be nice to her. She is just visiting us," Richter recalls the MD saying, as her 25 direct reports curiously stared back at her.

In retrospect, the MD might even be commended for having had language skills sufficient to so thoroughly and completely undermine a colleague in the space of a few short sentences, which was no small feat considering that he was able to reference Richter's youth, gender, and nationality while at the same time even summoning doubts about the permanence of her position.

While these words remain frozen in time for Richter, the lesson that she would carry forth from this role involved more their aftermath.

"LISTEN TO THE PEOPLE— LISTEN TO THEIR EXPECTATIONS AND LET THEM HELP YOU TO UNDERSTAND."

"This was my first leadership role, so my response was much more intuitive because at that age I had not taken any leadership seminars and didn't have any past experiences on which to draw," explains Richter, who says that her intuition told her to be a good listener.

"Listen to the people—listen to their expectations and let them help you to understand," she explains.

Fast-forward a number of years, and Richter is once more crossing borders—this time into Russia, where she is working as a senior finance professional for myToys, a large German e-commerce retailer.

Says Richter: "I had three months to set up the Russian entity, recruit the people, and make the goods available because we wanted to be operating by Christmas."

Today, Richter resides in Germany, where as CFO of Awin Global she applies her cross-border lessons to the global operations of Awin's quickly expanding affiliate marketing network. ■

Richter: As you can imagine, our business model is generating a lot of data. We are providing a lot of data to our partners, to our advertisers, and to our publishers. We have Tableau reports that are helping us to visualize all of what's happening, and we have a lot of BI reports to help reveal the different trends.

Just to give you one example of what we've done, during this coronavirus crisis we've built an industry tracker that is now helping us to better understand different segments and different regions and how are they performing. For instance, you can compare the retail businesses in Europe to the ones in U.S. and the ones in Brazil, which can be very helpful during times of crisis such as this.

We're now working to gather this type of information and data and create what I would call an "executive dashboard" because using your time to separately study five different sources or segments is not really practical. We wanted a condensed view that would include the five numbers that you want to be looking at, so that's what we are currently working on. ■

SCAN ME

📱 TO LISTEN

BENEATH THE HAZE OF COVID

GUEST CFO
JOHN THELER
Avetta

When John Theler stepped into the CFO office at SaaS developer Avetta last summer, among his list of priorities was the daunting task of better articulating supply chain hazards to management teams and industry at large.

Nine months later, Theler has no doubt added a number of items to his list of finance leader priorities, but his articulation task has become far less daunting. Not surprisingly, it seems that his thoughtful comments on the perils of poorly managed supply chains have paled in comparison to the high-wattage exposure that COVID-19 has suddenly brought to supply chains—an illuminating spotlight that Avetta and other suppliers of supply chain risk management services are now eager to put to work.

"ONE OF THE LONG-TERM EFFECTS OF THIS IS GOING TO BE A HIGHER SCRUTINY OF SUPPLY CHAINS GOING FORWARD."

"There clearly are some supply chain challenges and weaknesses that have already been uncovered through this crisis that we're in right now, and one of the long-term effects of this is going to be a higher scrutiny of supply chains going forward," explains Theler, who says that while many company boards have made supply chain risk management a bona fide component of their environmental sustainability and governance (ESG) efforts, COVID-19 is suddenly causing some firms to take a closer look at what's under the ESG hood.

"Our biggest competitors, frankly, are supply chains belonging to firms that just want to do it in their homegrown solution," says Theler, who quickly mentions the advantages of using Avetta's technology to address supply chain risk versus relying on typical in-house supply chain risk solutions.

There's little doubt that COVID-19 and its impact on industry at large will play a defining role in the careers of many finance leaders. For Theler and other CFOs, the pandemic is a house filled with obstacles and innovation where for every door that closes there's another that swings open. ∎

CFOTL: What other metrics or approaches do you use to measure business performance and customer purchases?

Theler: We look at a number of additional metrics, and some of them are unique to Avetta's situation. We are looking at connections for each of our clients and how many suppliers are they connected to. We consider the concept of nodal density, where some clients have a bunch of singular connections because those suppliers are unique only to that client. Other clients might be connected to a supplier, and that supplier might be connected to three or four other of our clients, and all of a sudden that supplier becomes a much more important supplier to us just because of the number of connections that they have. Again, we look at the number of connections between customers, clients, and suppliers, or their suppliers.

We look at the revenue per supplier. Going back to that concept of each supplier and their connections, and depending on how many are connected, we can assess our revenue as we get new insight into activations of new suppliers and clients and how many of those are activating. Because it's one thing to sign up a client and have them say, "Hey, we want you to help us to manage our supply chain," and it's another thing to have their supply chain actively signed up into our network to do it. So, we're looking at new activations. ∎

SCAN ME

📱 TO LISTEN

WHY RPA IS ATTRACTING MORE THAN CAPITAL

GUEST CFO
TOMER PINCHAS
Kryon

I n early 2020, following his arrival on a flight to Israel, Tomer Pinchas recalls receiving a startling text from the Israeli government. Having recently visited Italy, the text explained, passenger Pinchas must now agree to enter self-quarantine for a period two weeks. As CFO of Kryon—a Tel Aviv start-up specializing in Robotic Process Automation (RPA)—Pinchas, like most business travelers, was well aware of the recent spread of COVID-19. Still, the order to self-quarantine seemed aggressive to Pinchas, who at the time could not have imagined that in a few short weeks he would be sheltering in place with the rest of Israel.

"The actions taken by Israel were quite drastic and came pretty much a few weeks before the rest of the world, but what we learned during the process was that we can work anyplace—and sometimes we can be even more organized," says Pinchas, who believes that a new business environment is beginning to come into view.

"I REALLY BELIEVE THAT YOU NEED TO RAISE MONEY WHEN YOU CAN AND NOT NECESSARILY WHEN YOU NEED IT."

So far, the remote workforce is perhaps the new environment's most pronounced characteristic. However, some of the more interpersonal attributes of doing business may be compromised.

"Due to the fact that we work with enterprise customers and many things that we use to install are on-premise, we would often meet the customer face-to-face, so this will be kind of challenging in the new (environment)" explains Pinchas, who says that while face-to-face selling will likely be curtailed, Kryon's RPA offerings will find new traction among companies seeking new tools to help automate repetitive tasks and help them to better engage and respond to customer demands.

Fortunately, the RPA start-up closed on its latest round of financing within weeks of Israel sheltering in place.

"I really believe that you need to raise money when you can and not necessarily when you need it," remarks Pinchas, who believes that as long as a company has a strategy that it's prepared to execute—and not just an appetite for cash—the timing of a capital raise should not matter.

Says Pinchas: "Don't wait for the right time, because the majority of the time, there's no such thing. ■

CFOTL: What are your priorities as a finance leader over the next 12 months?

Pinchas: From my perspective, the question is not whether the pandemic is going to be over in three, six, or nine months. What we're trying to understand and predict, right now, is what this new world is going look like and what our opportunity is going to be in this new environment.

We are watching and forecasting. We started with one budget and adjusted accordingly to make sure that we manage our cash properly. I do believe that what is super-important under these circumstances is that you make the necessary adjustment so that you have sufficient cash—not for the next three, six, nine months, but more than that—while taking into consideration that there is going to be a slowdown, not necessarily because of your product but because the other side of the world may hesitate to make decisions. ■

SCAN ME
📱 TO LISTEN

A BANK INVESTING IN YOUR FINANCIAL HEALTH

GUEST CFO
THIBAULT FULCONIS
Varo Money

Earlier this year, when the FDIC approved fintech start-up Varo Money's application to become a national bank, Thibault Fulconis's latest CFO career chapter suddenly appeared to make perfect sense.

Still, it was only two years ago that Fulconis's entry into the land of fintech start-ups no doubt raised a few eyebrows among his former colleagues at BancWest Corp., where he most recently served as vice chairman and COO.

"I was coming from a position where I had about 3,000 direct reports when I was COO to an entity where I had three people reporting to me," says Fulconis, whose banking resume, rich with senior leadership roles, spans nearly 30 years with roots inside BancWest's parent company, BNP Paribas.

While certainly not the first banker to find a door-of-entry into the realm of fintech start-ups, Fulconis, in light of the FDIC's recent approval, became the first CFO of a fintech start-up that is able to hold customer deposits—much the same as in the world he left behind.

"YOU DON'T HAVE THE OCCASION TO OPEN A BANK FROM SCRATCH EVERY DAY. YOU HAVE TO BUILD EVERYTHING."

Until recently, fintech firms have partnered with community banks to actually hold customers' money, while start-ups like Varo have traditionally handled only the consumer interface and mobile app technology portion.

Who better than a seasoned banking leader to help architect a finance function capable of responding to the breadth of consumer activities on a national scale? "When I arrived at Varo, we were at version 76 of our financial model. Now, a year and a half later, we are at version 180," says Fulconis, who routinely expresses his fondness for Varo's nimbleness. ■

CFOTL: After 30 years in the large banking environment, what attracted you to Varo?

Fulconis: Well, you may not know that Varo is the first FinTech to have obtained the (regulatory approval) to become a bank, a full national bank. And so in the next 12 months my first challenge is, "Okay, let's open a bank." And that's what attracted me to Varo. You don't have the occasion to open a bank from scratch every day. So it's a bit of a dream come true. You have to build everything. So you don't have the old legacies and the old systems and so on. You can build from scratch. And you can say: "Okay, let's design something that would make for a really great finance function or risk function. So that's just a fantastic opportunity.

So we'll be opening our bank. And on top of that, we'll be opening a bank with a few million customers. So we already have human customers. So we'll be opening a bank, and we'd better have that bank work in both systems, work very well from day one. So that means that you have to have an asset liability management system in place, a regulatory reporting system in place. And of course your general ledger is your consolidation tool and so on. As you can imagine, we are doing a lot of stress testing on our data and what's happening.

CFOTL: How has COVID 19 impacted your efforts?

SCAN ME

📱 TO LISTEN

Fulconis: We tried to understand what's happening. Are people shopping more online? Yes, at the very beginning of the crisis, you had a big peak in groceries, just making sure that they have the food and the goods that they needed to live on. We saw that data and then we see people returning to a more normal life and starting to consume a little bit more online and expand their spending. ■

SHARPENING YOUR FIRM'S CUSTOMER...

GUEST CFO
DAVID WOODWORTH
insightsoftware

A t the age of 31, David Woodworth was offered CFO positions at two different firms. The first offer came from his then current employer, where as vice president of finance he was keenly aware of urgent challenges that the company's next CFO would need to address. The second offer came unsolicited from a smaller company in the same field, where he could expect to ease into the role and set the pace for his first 100 days.

"It was a hard decision, and one where you wish there was a silver bullet," says Woodworth, who opted to stay where he was, which was at a highly leveraged firm that had recently been taken private by a group of investors.

Woodworth's early chapter flies in the face of the widely expressed conundrum that to become a CFO, you have to be a CFO. However, in Woodworth's case, the price of entry to the CFO office was a cool head and an even keel—or at least being someone capable of working alongside a group of edgy investors.

"NOBODY HAS A CRYSTAL BALL, OBVIOUSLY, RIGHT? FOR FINANCE EXECUTIVES, WE HAVE TO PLAN FOR THE WORST."

"I had to embrace the role pretty quickly and operate in some unique environments," he adds.

Thinking back on his first CFO tour of duty, Woodworth concludes by saying, "The advice that I would like to give to someone stepping into a CFO role would be about how to prioritize and how to say 'no.'" ∎

CFOTL: As you improve your visibility into the business, what types of metrics are you adding to the mix? Are you relying on certain nonfinancial metrics such as the Net Promoter Score (NPS)?

Woodworth: The customer metrics that I sometimes refer to are really customer-specific internal dashboards. We don't look at a general NPS. We tend to look at very specific customer usage and customer support types of metrics. More broadly speaking, we focus very much on annual recurring revenue and corresponding margins by product type, as we've brought lots of products together. Certainly, in the COVID world, working capital is extremely important, too, as all finance execs are working to navigate their companies through this period of uncertainty.

Stepping back for a strategic, end-to-end view, certainly we look at LTV-to-CAC—that's long-term customer value to customer acquisition costs. We look at development spend and return in terms of our normal course and rhythm around assessing our development road map. We look at sales capacity and all those sorts of metrics that align with this kind of line of sight that finance has to look at the company from end to end.

Nobody has a crystal ball, obviously, right? For finance executives, we have to plan for the worst and have playbooks that reveal how to respond, whether from kind of lower impact conditions to severe ones. The way we've looked at it—and what our indications are as of today—is that we believe that this trough, for lack of a better word, or this negative impact is going to carry forward throughout 2020 and ultimately into 2021. We've run four different scenarios, just for our own plays, to figure out and determine the different actions that either we since have already taken or that we will take, depending upon certain milestones as we navigate through this period of uncertainty. ∎

SCAN ME

📱 TO LISTEN

THE FUNNEL: WHERE SALES & FINANCE MEET

GUEST CFO
ANDREW HICKS
Advanced

or every top sales leader who confides to friends that he or she is really a numbers freak at heart, there's an Andrew Hicks, who, as CFO of Advanced, would be just as apt to boast about a sales funnel innovation as he would about the adoption of a new accounting rule.

In fact, it would probably not surprise Hicks's past and present business colleagues to learn that when asked to identify a mentor from his past, Advanced's CFO chooses the head of sales for a former employer.

"It was because of this relationship that I first experienced an inkling of how people can think about the business differently and think differently about what drives value in the firm," explains Hicks, who found his mentor after being transferred to Austin from London by Misys, a UK-based software developer that today is part of Finastra.

"I had moved across the world, and the sales leader took me under his wing a bit as someone new in the U.S. who didn't really have family or friends nearby. Talking to him really piqued my interest in learning more about how the business worked," recalls Hicks, who would remain in the U.S. for nine years before being recruited for a CFO role back in London.

Along the way, Hicks's professional network became energized via a budding relationship with private equity firm Vista Equity Partners, which enlisted him as an advisor after Vista bought a portion of Misys's healthcare business. "Vista is continually working its network to find talent, and I was found by that means," says Hicks, whose CFO career chapter has to date been populated by multiple Vista-owned companies. ■

CFOTL: Tell us what metrics matter these days for Advanced?

Hicks: As my career has evolved, I've developed this passion for having finance information be driven from actually operating metrics. So, I try to challenge the traditional approach such that we are actually talking with operational colleagues around the things that they're doing and how they're running the business and having them so interlinked with the financial metrics that, frankly, the finance numbers take care of themselves. When I think about this, I'll be thinking about the sales pipeline and particularly bookings, which we think about with our own nomenclature here at Advanced. I'll be working with the CSO on what our pipeline coverage is looking like and what the conversion metrics are between the various stages in the funnel.

"THE FIRST THING WE DO IS HELP THE SALES TEAMS MAKE SURE THAT THEY'VE GOT THINGS IN THE RIGHT BUCKETS."

We've got a six-stage funnel that ranges from literally being a prospect on through to a closed deal. The first thing we do is help the sales teams make sure that they've got things in the right buckets because once they've got things in the right buckets, some of those 10 percent conversion rates become more reliable and more usable. It's all about engaging and communicating with and really challenging the sales organization around some of these, things, with a view toward optimizing performance. ■

SCAN ME

📱 TO LISTEN

UNLOCKING GREATER EFFICIENCIES

GUEST CFO
CHRIS SANDS
MineralTree

When Chris Sands accepted an investor relations position at a midsize health care firm, he did so with the understanding that he would be permitted to occasionally sink his teeth into some of the firm's growing FP&A challenges. Having a resume rich with investment banking experience, Sands was now determined to add some FP&A, a tour of duty that he viewed as a necessary prerequisite if he were going to advance down the CFO path.

Unbeknownst to Sands, his FP&A plate would shortly be overflowing following the acquisition of his new employer by Thermo Fisher Scientific of Waltham, Massachusetts. In the aftermath, Sands was enlisted to help lead the science giant's planning function, which allowed him to dine regularly on high-calorie planning and begin to consider his next opportunity.

Sands would open what he views as the third chapter of his career at MineralTree, after having been recruited by CEO Micah Remley, with whom Sands had worked earlier in his career.

"I COULD TELL FROM MY SEAT IN INVESTOR RELATIONS THAT INVESTORS WERE HAVING A HARD TIME UNDERSTANDING THE PERFORMANCE OF THE BUSINESS."

"Anytime a company is looking to hire a CFO, they inevitably ask for CFO experience as if people are born with it, so, for me, getting that experience became really important," observes Sands, who describes his decision to join MineralTree as a "no-brainer."

Looking back, Sands says that he would advise up-and-coming finance executives to actively seek out leadership mentors and not hesitate when it comes to expressing aspirations to become a CFO. Says Sands: "People aren't mind readers, but if they are a true mentor and know what your aspirations are, they will seek to enable you on your journey." ■

CFOTL: Tell us about a finance strategic moment of insight?

Sands: One finance strategic moment that immediately comes to mind actually occurred at the first job I took after I left JP Morgan. I had transitioned from Wall Street into industry and was running investor relations for a company called EnerNOC, which was a business that had evolved over time–but its reporting had not. I could tell from my seat in investor relations that investors were having a hard time understanding the performance of the business because the reporting hadn't caught up. I actually had the opportunity–which is a credit to my boss because he empowered me to do it–to lead an initiative inside the business to redesign the reporting and actually create segment reporting. This was hugely important from an IR perspective, but I would make the argument that it was even more important internally because we hadn't been looking at the business internally in that way. The old adage is that you can't manage what you can't measure.

That was such an important point in my career not only because it showed me the impact that you could have on a business from the finance seat, but also because when I had thought about my career evolving when I left JP Morgan and Wall Street to go into industry, I knew that I wanted to get into these skillsets. I knew that I had a great background in having come from investment banking and equity research, but I didn't necessarily have the confidence to know that I could run finance functions in a company. That particular project was one of the most confidence-inspiring moments in my career. ■

SCAN ME

📱 TO LISTEN

MAKING CUSTOMER OUTCOMES TOP OF MIND

GUEST CFO
VALERIE BURMAN
GuideSpark

Had Valerie Burman entered the CFO office a decade ago, you wonder whether the role would be as good a match for the accomplished finance executive as it appears to be today.

Back in 2007, after working nearly a decade in M&A as an investment banker, Burman exited a banking career to take on a corporate development role at Business Objects, a French software company that was soon to be acquired by SAP.

Post acquisition, Burman quickly found a groundswell of opportunities coming her way inside SAP, where she would serve in a variety of roles involving technology partnerships, business development, and product management.

"I WOULD SAY THAT WORKING FROM THOSE PERSPECTIVES... HAS REALLY LED ME TO A PLACE WHERE I CAN BE A CFO WITH A BUSINESS-MINDED, STRATEGIC APPROACH."

Fast-forward a few years, and we find Stanford Law graduate Burman serving as general counsel first to Mindjet and then to crowdsourcing innovation upstart Spigit.

"I would say that working from those perspectives—although it is a bit of a roundabout way to become a CFO—has really led me to a place where I can be a CFO with a business-minded, strategic approach," says Burman, who points out that along

the way, she was given the opportunity to closely observe the board room decision-making behind certain acquisitions designed to drive growth.

"The breadth of experiences that I have taken with me are not necessarily specific to my core finance role, but speak to my ability to understand cross-functionally what's important to my peers," Burman observes, while underscoring the growing cross-functional role that finance plays in business today.

For just as Burman's resume has evolved, so too has the role of CFO. ■

CFOTL: Tell us about your team and what steps you've taken to make an impact on the organization?

Burman: The areas that I've really been working to take the team to are more about not only making sure that we can adapt to change, but also that we're in a position to proactively drive that change through the organization. What this requires is that everybody on the team both is excellent their finance role and also understands the context in which we work—things like market dynamics, value proposition, competitive landscape, really understanding the product offerings deeply. I believe that ensuring that team members have the time and opportunity to get exposure to these things so that we all intuitively understand the business in the same way that our business partners do will really allow us not only to anticipate change but to drive it.

There are three ways in which we're pursuing this right now. First of all, I've instituted a regular team meeting in which we talk about company strategy and products and cascade learnings from various departments. The second is that the leaders on my team are now part of the extended leadership team at GuideSpark. We do regular cross-functional meetings where we work on initiatives that span various aspects of the company's business. Third, the various team members are now part of mentor circles that allow them to grow not just their individual finance skills, but also any other skills. ■

OPENING A SPIN-OFF'S LIBERATED CHAPTER

GUEST CFO
RAVI CHOPRA
SonicWall

 avi Chopra has built his career inside finance functions designed to serve growth-minded management. Such was the case in the late '90s when Chopra joined Cisco Systems, which at the time was experiencing 50% growth annually. Jump forward 10 years, and you'll find him busy leading the FP&A function for growth-driven Juniper Networks.

Asked to reflect back on a 25-year finance career, Chopra doesn't hesitate to cite his former employer. "I learned most of everything that I know today at Juniper," says Chopra, who quickly names Robyn Denholm, Juniper's former CFO and current Tesla chairman, as a present and former mentor. Still, when the door to the CFO office swung open for Chopra, the accomplished finance executive no doubt found his operations knowledge being put to the test.

In 2017, Chopra would exit Juniper Networks and take on the CFO role at SonicWall, a company that had neither a finance nor an HR organization after it split off from Dell, Inc., in late 2016. Dell had acquired SonicWall in 2012 but divested the business along with Quest Software as part of the larger Dell EMC integration.

Despite some missing parts, SonicWall arguably split off with something far more valuable intact: its brand name. Prior to being acquired by Dell, the cyber protection company had long since established itself as a leader in the small and midsize business space.

"It was just an amazing challenge, and I think that we have now come out on the other side of it rather well," explains Chopra, who believes that the speed with which SonicWall built its new infrastructure and achieved operational efficiencies allowed the firm to more quickly determine where to allocate capital. ∎

CFOTL: What was the opportunity that SonicWall represented to you and what did you see?

Chopra: Having (served) in different roles within finance, you get a really good appreciation of the different aspects of finance, the different aspects of a business. What's important today is that you want to be an operational CFO, which leads me to why I joined SonicWall. Obviously, there are lots of opportunities for many of us. We'll look at opportunities. We want to jump into those. I looked at many opportunities.

"WE NEEDED TO TURN THIS COMPANY AROUND – TO MAKE IT GROW BECAUSE IT HAD SORT OF STOPPED GROWING AS PART OF A BUSINESS UNIT WITHIN DELL."

With SonicWall, the biggest thing was that they had great technology. It was part of Dell, and in the divestiture, there were two things. One was that we almost had to build this company from scratch because it came with no infrastructure. All of our finance and IT infrastructure belonged to Dell, so it was almost like a start-up. We had to build the infrastructure again. It was a running company with hundreds of millions of dollars of revenue, and profits.

But at the same time, we needed to turn this company around – to make it grow because it had sort of stopped growing as part of a business unit within Dell. At the time of the divestiture, we were running on an ERP system that belonged to Dell, so we had to transfer into our own ERP system. I had probably three finance people of my own, so not only did I have to hire 30 to 35 people over the next six months, but also transfer our ERP over, get through our first full audit, and go through a capital-raising. ∎

SCAN ME

📱 TO LISTEN

ACHIEVING A STRATEGIC CAPITAL STRUCTURE

GUEST CFO
DAVID MOSS
INmune Bio

 mong the many lessons that David Moss has learned along the trajectory of his 25-year finance career, the one to which he refers simply as "the $3 million sweatshirt" is perhaps the most enduring.

Even after 20 years, Moss can't help but mention the sweatshirt bearing the logo of Pets.com, which he kept as a souvenir from an earlier career chapter involving a $3 million investment in the infamous dot-com retailing upstart.

Pets.com began operations in November 1998 and shut down in November 2000, becoming one of the more high-profile victims of the dot-com bubble. However, looking back, Moss says that while the economy's sudden gyrations certainly contributed to the firm's demise, other mistakes also came into play, including the filling of leadership roles with executives from large enterprise companies.

"WE WERE ABLE TO MAINTAIN A LOT OF INSIDER OWNERSHIP, BECAUSE WE'RE BIG BELIEVERS IN THIS BUSINESS."

"Someone from a large business often has a difficult time in adjusting to dynamic environments where you have to get your hands dirty and wear all of the hats and take the trash out," says Moss, who clearly has kept his appetite for investing in early-stage companies—especially inside the biotech realm, where he now resides as CFO and cofounder of INmune, a clinical-stage biopharmaceutical company. "We don't have a lot of complexity when it comes to how we built the business or the way that our accounting works, " adds Moss, who, along with two other cofounders, formulated a plan

TO LISTEN

to self-fund INmune. "Our mantra is to keep things simple," explains Moss, who says that the firm's capital structure underscores this philosophy, along with a preference for selling only common stock. ∎

CFTOL: Tell us about a finance strategic moment?

Moss: One very strategic moment in our business at INmune had to do with something that we did that was very unusual with regard to our financial situation. When companies go public, they typically go and hire an investment bank first. Then they go and draft all of their financial documents, and then they go and do their IPO and raise the money. We did the opposite here at INmune, which is probably very, very rare. We went and actually drafted our financial documents, got them approved by the regulatory authorities like the SEC and the NASDAQ, and then went and got our banks to do our capital raise. We did this because we wanted to be in the driver's seat.

We have this view that you want to drive your own destiny. You put yourself more in the driver's seat, show that you can do it, and then try to bring your financial players on board. That's what we did here.

As a result, what does this mean? There are positives and negatives with everything that you do. One positive is that because we drove the deal, it was mainly on our own terms. We also were able to maintain a lot of insider ownership, because we're big believers in this business. We believe in simplicity, so we wanted a simple cap structure. We didn't want to go into preferreds, we didn't want to go into convertible debt. We didn't want to go into warrants or anything like that. So, we kind of drove that on our own. A negative is that we weren't able to attract investor audiences as large as we would have if we had been more flexible in our terms and our deal structure. But all of this led to us ringing the bell on the NASDAQ, where we were actually the first biotech IPO of 2019. ∎

REPLACING THE IRON FIST WITH LISTENING

GUEST CFO
MIKE KASETA
Aerami Therapeutics

F ew megadeals within the past decade have perhaps received as many recurring kudos as the acquisition of Genzyme, of Cambridge, MA by France's biggest pharmaceutical company, Sanofi.

The marriage of Sanofi and Genzyme appears to have exceeded expectations, allowing all of those involved in minting the newly merged entity to rightfully keep a feather in their postmerger caps. Thus it was for Mike Kaseta, who in the wake of the merger found himself tasked with integrating the finance and IT functions of the two companies.

"It's probably the achievement that I'm most proud of in my career," explains Kaseta, who, after nearly a decade climbing the finance ranks inside Sanofi, exited the giant pharmaceutical company to stake a claim inside the realm of early-stage biotech, where today he is CFO of Aerami Therapeutics.

"WE HAVE TO GET OUR STORY OUT... WE HAVE TO GET IT OUT TO THE RIGHT PEOPLE AND REALLY ENGAGE WITH INVESTORS, ALLOWING THEM TO GET AS EXCITED ABOUT OUR STORY AS WE ARE."

Looking back, Kaseta believes that the greatest lessons he gleaned from the Sanofi–Genzyme merger were people-related: "There was no iron fist. We listened to employees. We understood. In the end, we had no control deficiencies, no comments from our external auditors, and the integration occurred in a timely manner."

Looking forward, Kaseta says that raising money now tops his list of CFO priorities at Aerami. "We have to get our story out," he adds. "We have to get it out to the right people and really engage with investors, allowing them to get as excited about our story as we are." ◼

CFOTL: Among Aerami's offerings is a device or inhaler that might offer value to other biotech companies – will partnerships be part of the greater strategy going forward?

Kaseta: We really look at ourselves as a development company, not a device company. We'd really look at an opportunity to look at compounds that could be novel new compounds or existing compounds that we feel would have a better method of action through an inhalation process. We are talking to potential strategic partners all the time about their portfolio, about potential compounds that we could partner with them on to use through our device. The flexibility of our company and the optionality of our company is something that we're really excited about. As we expand our portfolio and expand our pipeline, we really feel that the sky's the limit. There are a lot of therapeutic areas and a lot of disease states out there that have unmet needs in respiratory and cardiovascular and in metabolic disorders that we feel could really benefit from our device.

We're excited for the future. We feel that the capital that we raise and that we invest is most beneficial to our shareholders when it's invested in our science and development programs. We've remained very lean, so when we talk about how we engage investors and kind of go through things day to day, it's really a discussion with me, the CEO, and our chief development officer, who's really responsible for the overall development of our portfolio. We spend a lot of time together. We also spend a lot of time together with both current and potential investors, along with analysts. As we try to get the story of Aerami out there, we have very ambitious plans to develop multiple therapies. That requires capital, so for me success is going to be measured by our ability to raise capital. ◼

HAVE OTHERS TRANSMIT THE VISION

GUEST CFO
AMY SHELLY
OCC

A mong the experiences that Amy Shelly recalls as having helped to prepare her for a CFO role, the prep work for an upended IPO still looms large. Per the guidelines of the Securities and Exchange Commission (SEC), Shelly was tasked back in the late 1990s with gathering portions of the historical data that her employer—Hull Trading Company of Chicago—would need to disclose in an S1 filing prior to selling stock publicly.

"The weekend before the firm's partners were expecting to head out on the company's road show, Goldman Sachs came in and made Hull an offer that it just couldn't refuse," says Shelly, who swiftly became involved with the integration of Hull's operations into Goldman, an effort that she says eventually led her to work herself out of a job. "It was tough at the time but it ended up being okay," recalls Shelly, who believes that her involvement in Hull's S1 filing documents, along with the subsequent integration into Goldman, allowed her to glean unique insights into how business functions and departments engage and collaborate with one another.

"YOU DON'T HAVE CARRY EVERYTHING ON YOUR SHOULDERS. YOU NEED TO FIND PEOPLE WHO WILL HELP YOU TO SHARE AND TRANSMIT THE VISION."

After leaving Goldman, she held positions as vice president at ABN AMRO and vice president and controller for broker-dealer Chase Investment Services Corp. before stepping into the CFO role for the first time at Op-

tiver US LLC, a Dutch-owned options market-making firm. At Optiver, she lengthened her workdays and shortened her weekends. Looking back, Shelly today admits that she didn't delegate all that she should have. She explains: "You don't have carry everything on your shoulders. You need to find people who will help you to share and transmit the vision."

Three years into her latest CFO tour of duty with the Options Clearing Corporation (OCC) of Chicago, Shelly says that she's practicing what she preaches by empowering her team to share the vision for the business. At the OCC, this means adopting new technologies that can add some flexibility to the traditionally process-heavy organization. In the past, old systems and approaches placed limits on where and how decisions were made in the organization. Says Shelly: "I've always sought roles where I can help the business to make better decisions." ■

CFOTL: What numbers or metrics are always top of mind for you?

Shelly: Ninety-five percent of our revenue is driven by the volume that we clear, settle, and risk-manage every day, which is something that we don't control. We charge a clearing fee for our services, and as a low-cost service provider, I can't just charge any old amount. I'm very cognizant of how much volume we clear every day because our budget is based on an average daily volume rate. I'm also very cognizant of expenses. I'm okay with spending money, but I want to do it in a smart way. Last year, we began what we call our Renaissance initiative. It's a multiyear, multimillion-dollar program through which we are replacing our core technologies. The system that clears, settles, and risk-manages those positions every single day is about 20 years old, so we are looking to create a more modular, more agile system whereby we can increase our processing, we can better utilize the data that we receive every single day, and we can expand upon the risk management services that we provide. ■

SCAN ME

TO LISTEN

WHEN YOUR TACTIC IS THE STRATEGY

GUEST CFO
RAMAN KAPUR
Moogsoft

ears from now, if Silicon Valley's glitterati were ever to gather to celebrate the opening of a National Cloud Computing Museum, CFO Raman Kapur would make an excellent tour guide for the facility's finance wing. In fact, he could just chart the trajectory of his career from the dot-com bubble forward to help the world at large to better grasp how the cloud opportunity has grown and reshaped the finance business function.

"I'M PROUD TO SAY THAT I WAS AMONG THOSE WHO HELPED TO MAKE THE DECISION NOT TO CLOSE IT."

Our tour could begin at Intuit, the accounting software developer that Kapur joined in 2001 while seeking shelter from the dot-com bubble burst, where he quickly found his footing as a controller inside the company's fast-growing QuickBooks division. Looking back at his Intuit career chapter, Kapur recalls a loud internal debate that would ultimately determine the fate of a money-losing unit known at the time as "QuickBooks on the Web."

"I'm proud to say that I was among those who helped to make the decision not to close it. There was still a lot of talk around the question, 'Should we just close it down?,'" explains Kapur, who says that while the answer may seem obvious now, there was still room for debate back then, in light of the unit's early losses.

Kapur's controllership savvy propelled him into the cloud-friendly Big Data era at Splunk, where for nearly a decade he helped the data-hungry company to chart new growth paths as he himself advanced into the

role of vice president of finance—capping a tenure that exposed him to the likes of Godfrey Sullivan, a Silicon Valley stalwart who served as Splunk's chairman and CEO.

Today, Kapur recalls a quarterly meeting at which Sullivan surveyed Splunk's senior executives about the future direction of the company. According to Kapur, the discussion focused mainly on two areas where the company's offerings had been experiencing some extra traction.

Still, not everyone viewed the new areas of traction as resources-worthy, at which point Sullivan remarked: "Your successful tactic becomes your strategy"—an insight that Sullivan used to open the minds of his management team and which led the company to double down on one of the two areas – a space Splunk has since grown exponentially.

Meanwhile, Kapur is able to quickly validate the insight as he reflects back on his own experiences: "More often than not, you try a couple of things and one of them becomes the bigger part of your business," says Kapur, who exited Splunk in 2018 to step into the CFO office at Moogsoft. ∎

CFOTL: When we ask you about metrics that are top of mind – we suspect you will likely tell us about annual renewable revenue (ARR) and lifetime customer value – but can you be more specific for us?

Kapur: One of our key metrics is upsell. How much upsell do you get out of a customer? This helps you to calculate the lifetime value of the customer. Why is this so important? Because if you want to have a business that grows fast, you cannot land customers fast enough to grow at 50%, 60%. The only way to do it is to have 80% of the business come through upsell. Eighty percent of the growth comes through upsell and the other 20% comes through new business. If you have a business model wherein once you acquire a customer, the customer buys more and more every year, that is a very sustainable business model that eventually will deliver great results because (1) your cost of doing business as you become a bigger company is lower, and (2) you are selling more software to existing customers instead of having to spend money to acquire new ones. ∎

SCAN ME

📱 TO LISTEN

ACHIEVING ONGOING CUSTOMER VALUE

GUEST CFO
DAVID ERTEL
Vizient

number of years back, when the management of Vizient began evaluating a list of candidates for future CFO, the odds were that David Ertel would top the list.

Still, with no accounting degree and no real audit experience, Ertel might have appeared to some to be somewhat of a dark horse candidate. However, among those who had crossed paths with him during his 25-year investment banking career (Morgan Stanley, Paine Webber) or as he tracked and studied healthcare finances as a policy analyst for New Jersey's Department of Human Services, few would have questioned the executive's enduring focus on healthcare finance.

"ONE OF THE REASONS THAT THIS POSITION WAS ATTRACTIVE TO ME WAS THAT I WOULD BE ABLE TO BRING AN OUTSIDE-IN VIEW INTO THE COMPANY AND ITS GROWTH."

Ertel had in fact focused his career lens even before heading to Wall Street, having earned a combined MBA/MPH from Columbia University.

"One of the reasons that this position was attractive to me was that I would be able to bring an outside-in view into the company and its growth," explains Ertel, who characterizes his perspective as being different from that of a "homegrown CFO."

As for Vizient, Ertel says that the membber-owned healthcare services company has a "stickiness" with its customers that most other businesses can't match. "Our customers are pretty much online with us 24/7, so it's up to us to make certain that all of those touch points are working and that in the event something goes down, we've got a plan to get back up very quickly," he explains. ■

CFOTL: Tell us about your top of mind metrics?

Ertel: Largely defined, most of Vizient's revenue is—I'm going to put it in air quotes—"subscription-oriented." Some of it is literal subscriptions, whether SaaS or other offerings, but much of it is driven by multiyear contracts that operate as subscription services, such as for clinical data or for a group purchasing organization. While on the one hand this provides great visibility on future revenue, the challenge with these types of organizations is to not just sit back and rest on your laurels. What offerings enhancements do you put forward to really take advantage of the built-in stickiness that you have because it's either a contract or a subscription that serves as a contract? How do you really enhance something so that you're providing value to those customers on an ongoing basis by improving the offerings?

That's a good starting point, but it doesn't change the dynamic of the fact that you have to be out there every day as a company, whether you're on the back office or CFO side of the equation or you're out with customers. I think that it's an important point for a company like this to understand and rise to that challenge. As far as metrics go, it's revenue per customer, it's margin per customer, it's overall EBITDA margin when you look at financial statistics, but then it's also member retention.

CFOTL: What are your priorities for the next 12 months?

Ertel: Well, the first would be achieving our budget... It's one year of a multi-year plan, but that multiyear plan is really the focus of the next year. How do we gain the seeds for success in years two, three, four, five, and out into the future? ■

SCAN ME

📱 TO LISTEN

ESTABLISHING YOUR WORK ETHOS

GUEST CFO
BEA ORDONEZ
OTC Markets Group, Inc.

P erhaps, unlike most of her professional peers, when Bea Ordonez interviewed for the first time for a CFO role, she got the job. At the time, perhaps no one was more surprised than Ordonez, whose finance resume—while impressive for a 26-year-old—still lacked a number of C-suite prerequisites. Twenty years later, she still resides in the C-Suite, having filled a number of consecutive CFO and COO roles over the years.

"I INTERVIEWED, LANDED THE ROLE, AND THEN WORKED REALLY, REALLY HARD TO LEARN THE BUSINESS FROM THE GROUND UP."

Nonetheless, she credits her first CFO tour of duty with having opened the door for everything that has followed.

"On paper, at least, I was woefully underqualified for the job. I interviewed, landed the role, and then worked really, really hard to learn the business from the ground up," says Ordonez, whose first CFO stint was with a joint venture originally formed with Bloomberg Tradebook known as G-Trade. Located on the island of Bermuda, the broker-dealer start-up no doubt found Ordonez an attractive hire in part because she was at the time an island resident.

Still, for all of those trying to decode shortcuts to the C-suite or uncover a coveted secret behind becoming a 26-year-old CFO, we'd wager that Ordonez's words "worked really, really hard" perhaps best reveal her world of both today and 20 years ago.

As G-Trade grew, Ordonez became tasked with quickly adding talent to help answer the organization's growing demand for financial and operational support.

"We were providing support for trading activities across close to 90 global markets and at the same time building a culture and creating a work ethic that even to this day I am very proud of," recalls Ordonez, while once more drawing our attention to her unwavering appetite for the work itself.
"At times in my career, I didn't have any personal life, and what time I did have, I used for sleeping," confides Ordonez, who adds that today—more than ever before—she aspires to achieving a positive work/life balance. ■

CFOTL: Tell us about this business and its unique offerings?

Ordonez: In the simplest terms, we operate a trading market for about 10,000 public companies. We operate three business lines. One is a trading business. We operate two SEC-registered alternative trading systems. What those platforms do is allow broker-dealers to connect and to efficiently trade those 10,000 securities that are on our platform. The second business line is a suite of products that we provide to the companies, that is, to issuers. What we're doing here–again, in very simple terms–is providing them with access to all of the benefits of a public trading market at a much lower cost and with much less complexity. Finally, just as with an exchange, those first two business lines generate a lot of proprietary market data, such as pricing information, company data, and so on.

You can see that just like an exchange, we serve a diverse sector of the market. We serve about 100 broker-dealers who trade on our platform. We have more than 10,000 companies, which are very, very diverse. We have more than 6,000 global companies, non-U.S. firms, including Roche, Adidas, Heineken, Marks & Spencer, Hugo Boss, and so on. ■

SCAN ME

📱 TO LISTEN

CHAMPIONING CASH FLOWS TO DISARM COVID

GUEST CFO
HILLA SFERRUZZA
Meritage Homes

W hen it comes to protecting the business from the bite of the pandemic, Meritage Homes CFO Hilla Sferruzza makes it clear that her primary focus remains on cash flow and preserving whatever she can of it to help the home builder weather what lies ahead.

"It's a pretty long cycle, and there is a substantial cash outlay at the start of the life of a community versus at the tail end, which is really when it is cash flow positive," reports Sferuzza, who estimates that the cash outlays for most of Meritage's communities run two to three years before becoming cash flow positive.

"We have to buy the land, which is expensive, and we have to develop the land, which is expensive. We have to build the models and then we have to build the homes," adds Sferruzza, whose top-of-mind cash flow priorities are not unlike those of other finance leaders whose businesses were pursuing steep growth trajectories.

Still, Sferruzza explains that "it's actually not as stressful a scenario for us as it might appear to be. We become extremely cash accretive during a downturn because we stop spending money on new land, and everything on our balance sheet converts to cash." ∎

CFOTL: What will distinguish your CFO tenure at Meritage?

Sferruzza: I love the forecasting and budgeting component of the role. I think it allows us to steer the ship. This is a long (cycle) business. If you think about when you buy land and then you develop it and then you build a model and then you build all the homes and then you start selling, it's a very long trajectory. So, having a confident outlook

on cash, I think is critical. If you are out of cash, obviously it's problematic. You're going to (opt) out of communities and if you have too much cash, it's a wasted opportunity. You could have done more. So I think we've really, as a team here and I don't want to say I, because I have an amazing team. Some of them have been with me the entire 14 years. I have one of the longest tenures in my group, which I'm extremely proud of.

"IT'S PROBABLY ONE OF MY FAVORITE ACCOMPLISHMENTS OF MY CAREER HERE, MY TENURE WITH MY TEAM."

It's probably one of my favorite accomplishments of my career here, my tenure with my team. We really have focused on tightening and improving our understanding of the cashflow process in our business and I really feel that's allowed us to get comfortable with the pre-building of the inventory, right?

It's very expensive to build homes, so if you think back to what we just talked about on having the inventory, that's ready for our customer to walk into, that's a very expensive proposition, right? To have a whole bunch of homes ready in 250 plus communities across the country.

So you can only do that if you're confident that your team has correctly helped you in assessing the cash flows. And I think we've put up heightened focus on that process.

And then the other component is again, just the integration of ops into accounting and finance. And for me, I always tell my team, because the dollars that we deal with in home building are so large. And I always have to remind them that's dollars, that's just not numbers, right? Those billions are dollars. So let's make sure that we understand all the components of what goes into it. ∎

SCAN ME

📱 TO LISTEN

CHARTING YOUR COURSE TO SURVIVE AND THRIVE

GUEST CFO
AMIR JAFARI
Reputation.com

W hen Amir Jafari looks back and reflects on his path to the CFO office, he includes two character traits that have arguably long distinguished finance leaders from other functional leaders.

"We in finance have high levels of accountability and integrity, and these are the things that we're able to then transpose in terms of what we do and how we are able to lead as CFOs," explains Jafari, who says that it was his ability to "transpose" these traits during a recent career chapter at ServiceNow that allowed him to ultimately gain the leadership experience required to step into a CFO role at Reputation.com.

> ## "THE BIGGEST TWIST IN MY ENTIRE LIFE—AND ONE THAT I THINK ULTIMATELY HELPED ME TO PREPARE FOR A CFO ROLE—IS THAT I HAD A CHANCE TO BE THE GENERAL MANAGER OF A BUSINESS UNIT. "

"I landed at ServiceNow as their corporate controller, but the biggest twist in my entire life—and one that I think ultimately helped me to prepare for a CFO role—is that I had a chance to be the general manager of a business unit," explains Jafari, who notes that his GM tour of duty was rooted in the creation of two applications that ultimately evolved into a business unit.

"Being able to lead a product management team,

an engineering team, a design and go-to-market team is very different from my past assignments and has really helped to round out the core elements of what we do in traditional finance," comments Jafari.

While there's little doubt that Jafari's ascent into leadership roles was aided by more than accountability and integrity, he credits his finance career track for helping to preserve and nourish these traits along the way, allowing him to more confidently assume leadership roles when opportunities arrived. ■

CFOTL: What are some of the economic indicators that you are watching these days?

Jafari: We really want to look at this through the lens of our customers to make sure that we are beyond empathetic and have compassion for each of their respective industries. In healthcare—when healthcare reopens back up to a normal process—we'll be looking at the folks who serve the elderly, or elective surgeries, or wherever the need may be. Perhaps it's the dental shops across the U.S., as an example: What are the key stats for when they can open from an economic perspective?

At a macro level, of course, there's unemployment. There are a lot of key stats there, some of which are lagging. But we view things more in terms of industry by industry to see what's happening.

We're in a world that is highly abnormal. There's a "sense of pause" that's been created. For me, this is a unique opportunity because when the world is standing still, we have the ability right now to validate our vision. We believe strongly in our purpose—that this whole notion of reputation matters—so we want to refine our strategy. We want to be able to come out of this and thrive. That's what we're doing today. We're refining our strategy with regard to COVID. We have looked at various scenarios. But also I think it's important for people to step back and understand what the world is going to look like post-COVID. ■

SCAN ME

📱 TO LISTEN

GETTING A READ ON ECONOMIC RECOVERY

GUEST CFO
MICHAEL BORRECA
LYNX Franchising

F inance leaders who remain skeptical of the prospects for economic recovery any time soon may want to consult LYNX Franchising CFO Michael Borreca.

"I don't think that it's going to take us long to get back to March 2020 sales levels," says Borreca, who doesn't hesitate to credit three nontraditional metrics for influencing his current thinking on the subject.

"THE MORE OUR FRANCHISE NETWORK IS BUYING DISINFECTANTS, THE MORE THIS MEANS THAT MORE BUSINESSES ARE STARTING TO REOPEN."

The first is the volume of disinfectant currently being purchased by franchisees of JAN-PRO—owned by LYNX—which boasts of being the largest commercial cleaning franchiser in the country, with over 8,000 small business owners.

"The more our franchise network is buying disinfectants, the more this means that more businesses are starting to reopen. They are doing a deep clean ahead of time, and then customers are being welcomed in," says Borreca, who counts the lengthening commuting times surrounding LYNX's hometown of Atlanta, Georgia, as yet another unconventional metric pointing now toward a recovery.

The third metric influencing Borreca's upbeat economic outlook is the growing digital sales leads for Intelligent Office, a virtual office business that LYNX acquired early last year. In addition to its à la carte virtual office assistant services, Intelligent Office also provides businesses access to furnished office spaces and meeting rooms. "Folks are looking for private space where they can go to get out of the house and work, but ours is not an open coworking environment," explains Borreca, who says that as leases expire, the pandemic is already leading many companies to rethink how they use and pay for space. ■

CFOTL: What are some of the opportunities that you see taking shape in this new environment?

Borreca: I'm in a very enviable situation in that I have brands such as JAN-PRO and Intelligent Office that all companies of any size can really benefit from. My number one goal is taking advantage of this returning market and adding what maybe would have been, pre-COVID, special services or special items as recurring revenue solutions for our end customers and our businesses. Number two: We acquired Intelligent Office as part of building the LYNX Franchising concept, so we'll be continuing down the M&A front and looking for the right brands to keep adding to and building the LYNX Franchising enterprise. We'll be looking for brands that fit our culture and brands that fit our other brands for cross-selling and added synergies. Last, we'll be trying to capture new customers who previously would have been dismissive of our offerings prior to COVID. I think that historically we've had some customers, such as state governments, who wouldn't disinfect their subway cars or buses on a daily basis. Now they are interested in doing this, and we can do it at a very cost-effective price.

SCAN ME
▢ TO LISTEN

On the Intelligent Office side, we had historically gone after smaller businesses and entrepreneurs, but I think that there are mid-tier companies that are similar in size to LYNX Franchising who can take advantage of our offering from the Intelligent Office side and not have to hire W-2 employees to be customer service representatives or executive admin assistants. ■

ALL EYES ON RECOVERY INDICATORS

GUEST CFO
JOHN BONNEY
Harness

W hen John Bonney joined San Francisco-based Harness a little more than a year ago, he became not only the company's first CFO but also its first finance hire.

"For me, this was the first time that I came into a role with a blank slate—it was at Ground Zero," explains Bonney, who says that the software start-up specializing in the automation of software applications delivery had theretofore been outsourcing its finance, legal and IT functions.

Initially, he recalls, he was somewhat doubtful that he was good match for such an early-stage firm—and especially one with such meager internal operations.

However, he became intrigued by the challenge that Harness CEO Jyoti Bansal put before him.

Looking back, Bonney says that he knew that "we could become really big, and here was a chance to set the foundation right."

"WHEN A COMPANY HAS RAISED CAPITAL AND THE QUESTION BECOMES 'WHERE DO YOU PUT THAT CAPITAL?,' THE CFO AND FP&A TEAM HAVE TO IMPACT THIS AND MONITOR IT."

Within 5 months, Bonney relates, he had fielded a team of roughly eight people, including a controller, an FP&A leader, and department heads for legal and IT.

"Generally, when companies are really small, it doesn't always make financial sense to have people in-house, but as you grow to 100 people and beyond, what you quickly begin to experience are bottlenecks impacting responsiveness to IT needs or legal bills that are beginning to balloon," explains Bonney, who adds that positions outside the finance realm were filled first, with the FP&A hire a more recent addition to the team.

Says Bonney: "When a company has raised capital and the question becomes 'Where do you put that capital?,' the CFO and FP&A team have to impact this and monitor it."

Meanwhile, as Harness scales, the company has prioritized the use of new applications and technologies to perform work traditionally completed by back office hires. For example, Bonney says, Harness did not hesitate to adopt applications vendor Airbase of San Francisco to manage its companywide credit card spending and expense management. Asked to reflect on his first year as CFO of Harness and his Ground Zero "to do" list. Bonney quips: "12 months gone by in a blink of an eye." ■

CFOTL: What are your priorities as a finance leader over the next 12 months?

Bonney: While running any business, you've got to track the pulse of it all the time. Now more than ever—when it's a very uncertain time—it's important for a business not to overreact to what's going on but to track the pulse of the business and understand the trends. Right now, we're monitoring things weekly, daily, and we're looking at trends and leading indicators to consider what they mean for the pipeline. What are we seeing with our customers' usage? We're really diving in now to focus on and understand our customers. How quickly are they up and adopting our product? Where did they stumble, or where did they not? We're using a lot of things to constantly refine our operating cadence, how we build our product, and how we serve the customer. ■

WHEN IT'S TIME FOR A FIRE DRILL

GUEST CFO
GORDON STUART
Unit4

In the late 1980s, when Gordon Stuart exited a 4-year stint as an auditor with Price Waterhouse, he bid accounting farewell—or at least he did until he stepped into a CFO role roughly a dozen years later.

Ever since, he has occupied multiple CFO roles, helping to remove any doubt about his finance and accounting orientation.

Still, Stuart's appetite for broader business experiences during the early part of his career set him apart from many of his finance leader peers. During the 1990s, as a senior engagement manager for strategy consulting firm McKinsey & Company, he found job satisfaction across a variety of industries.

"IT TAUGHT ME AN AWFUL LOT ABOUT HOW TO WORK WITH TEAMS AND UNDERSTAND BUSINESSES AND BUSINESS MODELS, AS WELL AS HOW TO COMMUNICATE WITH OTHERS."

Asked what originally led him to join McKinsey rather than take on a more traditional corporate finance role, Stuart says that "the opportunity that I saw would allow somebody who's naturally curious about business to build a better set of capabilities, frameworks, experiences, and connections to further their career."

Looking back, Stuart says that his biggest take-away from his 6 years with McKinsey

involved the approach that McKinsey uses while serving clients.

"It taught me an awful lot about how to work with teams and rapidly assimilate and understand businesses and business models, as well as how to communicate with others. In fact, I think that this was probably one of the key learnings," says Stuart, who would leave the strategy house in 1998 to become director of strategy for Dell Europe, where he would ultimately set up and lead the technology company's Web hosting business for Europe.

"Our timing was unfortunate because the dotcom collapse of 2000 kind of reset priorities within Dell, and that's when my CFO career began," explains Stuart, who left Dell after the CEO of a UK software company (and former McKinsey colleague) convinced him to accept the software firm's finance leadership role. "I never set out with an ambition to be a CFO, but as time passed, I kind of realized that if you pick the right business and it lines up with your interests, CFOs influence a lot of what happens in a business. And having an impact is very satisfying," he explains. ∎

CFOTL: Are there certain metrics that you want to bring more attention to across the organization?

Stuart: One of the by-products of our SaaS migration is that it's enabling me to do something that I've been trying unsuccessfully to do for 20 years, which is to get the business to look past the end of the year. Nothing drives me to distraction more than the 31st of December. It's the end of the world as far as most people are concerned. I keep making the point that when you switch your computer off on the 31st and then you come back on the 2nd of January, it's the same stuff in your mailbox. It's the same deals that you're working on.

We're trying to use the whole ARR model to get people to think further ahead in their planning. We had a chat earlier this morning about our budget process for 2021. I said, "We can start it now because we know from our 3-year plan what we want our cost run rate to look like and what we want our ARR for our recurring business to look like. So all that we've got to do is to plot the course. ∎

WHEN FINANCE SINGS A NEW TUNE

GUEST CFO
JOHN CAPPADONA
School of Rock

U nlike the music artists and instructors recruited by School of Rock to provide music lessons at its 270 locations around the globe, John Cappadona was first hired by the firm to provide a crash course in accounting.

"The day I joined, my controller and I walked through the door together not knowing anything," explains Cappadona, who stepped into the CFO role at School of Rock shortly after its CEO, Rob Price, moved the music lesson provider's headquarters to the Boston area.

"WE WOULDN'T HAVE KNOWN THAT WE WERE GOING TO RUN INTO AN ICEBERG UNTIL WE HIT IT."

Says Cappadona: "For the first couple of months, it took us almost 25 days to close the books—and we needed to shorten that number in order to start making decisions sooner."

Next, Cappadona set out to enhance the management team's visibility into the business.

"We wouldn't have known that we were going to run into an iceberg until we hit it," comments Cappadona, who adds that while his team did not come across any icebergs, the company's sales reporting numbers were just not visible enough.

After making a number of accountant hires, Cappadona says, he became focused on developing School of Rock's FP&A function to better reveal the performance at its 270 locations—49 of which were company-owned. The company's finance team keeps a close eye on the number of new students as well as School of Rock's net promoter score.

Still, when it comes to measuring customer behavior, Cappadona believes that as a consequence of the pandemic, School of Rock's lines of sight into customer behaviors are poised to grow rapidly.

"We are deriving 100 percent of our revenue right now from something that did not exist 2 months ago. We were an in-person education business. We had to pivot immediately to deliver a remote solution," says Cappadona, who recorded an episode with CFO Thought Leader in May 2020.

As it turns out, a customer lesson delivered remotely would appear to be a nice complement to School of Rock's in-person lessons.

Notes Cappadona: "At the end of the day, the mission is really the same—and it's our sense of community that sets us apart." ■

CFOTL: Tell us about a finance strategic moment...

Cappadona: I'll tell you about my time at WB Mason, where I was really charged with bringing up the FP&A department, with creating it. Previously, they really hadn't had the sort of financial insights coming forth that they needed. What really comes to mind is Hurricane Sandy, or Superstorm Sandy, which hit the East Coast hard. WB Mason was primarily focused in the Northeast, so pretty much all of our operations were out of business for several days. We had to quickly engage our forecast models, and there were some tough decisions that we had to make. We had to shore up costs because we had bank covenants that we had to maintain, and we had to make sure that given the decreased revenue, our cost structure was going to be fine.

SCAN ME

📱 TO LISTEN

This was one of those strategic moments when we had to look ahead to say, "Well, when are these businesses going to be coming back?" It was very similar to what we're facing today with the pandemic. Now I'm digging back into my bag of tricks just as I did seven or eight years ago when I was trying to model things out. There was a lot of pressure to do the work and get the answers right. ■

LEVERAGING THE VALUE OF CULTURE

GUEST CFO
WILL COSTOLNICK
Hire Dynamics

Years from now, when Will Costolnick thinks back to the start of his CFO career, he will likely count the 12 months that preceded his appointment as CFO of Hire Dynamics as part of the same chapter, for—not unlike many of his CFO peers—Costolnick first found his footing at his new employer by slipping into a vice president of finance role for a year or two.

In Costolnick's case, the interim role lasted 12 months, or just long enough for Hire Dynamics to reformulate its management ranks and expand its C-suite.

"SITTING IN A ROOM WITH THE LEADERS FROM PRODUCT DEVELOPMENT, MARKETING, AND SALES, I GOT TO OBSERVE THEM AS THEY LOOKED AT THESE TARGETS STRATEGICALLY."

Still, Costolnick hit the ground running by using his interim credentials to begin putting in place processes that would accommodate new growth, which was indeed a priority for satiating the staffing firm's newfound appetite for acquisitions.

Four years ago, Hire Dynamics had but 10 offices in the Southeast; today, this number is 47. The growing office numbers follow a recent spurt of deal-making by Hire Dynamics, which today boasts of being the Southeast's second largest commercial staffing firm. Clearly, the timing of Costolnick's arrival was no accident. Moreover, the firm's newly charged CFO had spent four of his previous six years evaluating acquisition targets for LexisNexis Risk Solutions.

"We looked at 40 acquisitions during that period and closed on eight," explains Costolnick, who served as lead finance analyst for the company's internal mergers and acquisitions group.

"I think that this was really a pivotal moment for me. I would be sitting in a room with the leaders from product development, marketing, and sales, and I got to observe them as they looked at these targets strategically," says Costolnick, who later served as director of finance for the Atlanta-based firm.

While acquisition targets are no doubt part of Costolnick's world these days, so too are the processes and technologies that in the future will permit Hire Dynamics to satisfy the demands of an organization many times its present size. ■

CFOTL: You join Hire Dynamics as a vice president of finance and in short order you enter the CFO office. This is not an unusual approach, but can you retrace your initial steps for us?

Costolnick: My first role after walking in the door was to take this team that was kind of disconnected and working in their own silos and bring them together. We created a true FP&A team that hadn't existed before, and we created a dedicated payroll team and a collections team. All of these teams at first hadn't existed. You had people wearing multiple hats, but no one specializing in anything. This was my first task: to just simply look at roles and responsibilities and build out these core teams that could scale with the business.

SCAN ME

📱 TO LISTEN

Within the first year, we had rolled out about four robots to help to automate the highly transactional processes—the repetitive day-to-day stuff—so that we could take them off the finance team's work list in order to put more value-add time back into their day. We implemented dashboards and got rid of manual reporting altogether. We said, "Look, if we're going to scale this business, we need to use technology." ■

OPENING YOUR ACQUISITION CHAPTER

GUEST CFO
JODY CIRE
AllCloud

 When the Sarbanes–Oxley Act was enacted 18 years ago, it required the Securities and Exchange Commission to create regulations to define how companies should comply with it—a mandate that would end up impacting the careers of finance professionals well into the future.

Finance leader Jody Cire was one such professional. Back in 2010, Cire found himself in Boulder, Colorado, after having been relocated from a role in Germany as KPMG's lead audit manager for SAP AG. In light of his recent large enterprise experience, KPMG had been eager to assign Cire stateside in order to scratch the Sarbox itch of some of its largest customers.

Within a year, Cire found himself knee-deep in massive Sarbox compliance projects with a number of prestigious clients.

Still, something was missing.

Says Cire: "It just wasn't where my personality or where my curiosity really thrived. I just didn't enjoy it and began to express that."

Meanwhile, his appetite for assignments involving start-ups and high-growth firms had never wavered, allowing him to confidently exit KPMG and step into a corporate role as vice president of finance and accounting for Boulder-based cybersecurity firm LogRhythm.

During most of his career, Cire's accounting and technical knowledge had made him a standout. At LogRhythm, he would quickly be challenged in new and different areas. Chief among them was helping the company to develop a successful exit strategy, which eventually was realized in 2018 when it was acquired by private equity firm Thoma Bravo. "We were already over $200 million—Thoma Bravo wanted some fresh blood and new management because there had to be some housecleaning and stripping out of costs," says Cire, who served as LogRhythm's interim CFO before stepping into the CFO office at cloud solutions provider AllCloud early last year. ∎

Cire: We established a 2020 budget that was approved when we had a board of directors meeting on January 6. We were 6 days into 2020, and we already had an approved budget. I've never been able to accomplish a budget approval so fast in my life. Meanwhile, we also had an internal management plan. Unfortunately, in 2020, this doesn't win you any prizes because within 6 weeks the world had completely changed. Right? So, in March, we suddenly found ourselves in a reforecasting period involving the general management of our regions, as well as the CEO and myself and my FP&A team. Together we had look at what we saw and what amount of cutting we might need to do.

"WE'VE GOT PEOPLE WHO HAVE BUILT AND SOLD BUSINESSES BEFORE, SO WE ARE VIEWED AS A GOOD PLATFORM PLAY FOR ADDITIONAL ACQUISITIONS."

When it comes to our priorities going forward, we get a lot of inbound interest from potential investors. What they like about AllCloud as a company is that we have a senior leadership team that is structured very well. We've got people who have built and sold businesses before, so we are viewed as a good platform play for additional acquisitions. But to do this, there has to be a good succession plan. There have to be good people below me, so I have to continued to build my teams and to build systems that allow for easy integration. ∎

MINDING YOUR FINANCIAL PS AND QS

GUEST CFO
MATT ELLIS
Verizon

I t's a story that Verizon CFO Matt Ellis seems to enjoy telling and one that he has undoubtedly related more than once before.

One evening while in high school, Ellis was working at the fish counter of a local supermarket when he received some feedback from the store manager.

Earlier in the day, the man had asked Ellis to clean a number of shelves beside the counter, but Ellis had soon become busy with fish patrons and hadn't been able to complete the task.

"RANTING AND RAVING IS NOT THE WAY TO GET THROUGH TO PEOPLE."

More than 30 years later, Ellis easily retrieves the store manager's words: "I'm not disappointed that you didn't get it done—I know that you were busy with your normal stuff. What disappoints me is that if you had only told me, I could have arranged to have someone else to do it."

This is a classic management lesson that many business leaders have communicated before, but when Ellis presents it, the message is endowed with renewed relevance for finance.

It is easy for us to imagine Ellis retrieving the store manager's lesson to enlighten a young finance analyst—or perhaps even his own approach as he prepares to brief Verizon board members on looming strategy snags.

"This taught me two things: One was the value of communicating bad news as early as possible, and the second lesson was the way in which he gave feedback—ranting and raving

is not the way to get through to people," explains Ellis, who even today seems to muster genuine appreciation for—and perhaps even marvel at—the store manager's evenhanded demeanor.

It's not surprising that Ellis shares a lesson that reveals the power of communication in finance. This is a skill that you suspect he acquired early in his career and that has contributed to his ongoing ascent in responsibility and reward.

Having worked beside CFOs at Tyson Foods and Verizon for nearly a decade, Ellis arguably understood the CFO role better than most when he eventually became a CFO himself, at Verizon.

Asked what advice he would have given himself in the first week of his tenure, Ellis responds that the parts of the CFO role about which he was most uncertain turned out to be those that up to that point had not been part of his experience.

"It's the interactions with the other members of the senior leadership team that become different," he reports. "It's the importance of one-on-one communication—not the group meetings to which I had become accustomed before." Here, too, Ellis's communication skills have no doubt served him well. ∎

CFOTL: How is finance helping to create greater visibility into Verizon's business?

Ellis: One of the things that we've been spending time on—and that we will continue to do—is to really try to create an increased level of understanding of the relationship between what drives revenue, cost, and how much of the cost is fixed versus variable.

As the different teams have looked at the different parts of the business, this has really forced us to think about our spending in a different way. We don't have a finished product on this by any means, but we're really trying to continue to provide more transparency on what drives cost, what causes cost to happen, and as you do this, some unexpected things fall out. People say, "I didn't realize that we did this." ∎

AN ACQUISITIVE STATE OF MIND

GUEST CFO
JON NGUYEN
Kyriba

 on Nguyen got his first taste of M&A-related work in the early to mid-2000s when he served as the vice president of finance partner for the auto lending unit of HSBC.

"In consumer lending, you end up doing a lot of portfolio purchases rather than equity ones, but I have become more involved in the execution of deals over the past 8 years," says Nguyen, who sees the past 8 years as a standout chapter in his career that has allowed him to certify his M&A credentials and exposed the path to the CFO office.

"IT'S INTERESTING HOW LIFE CAN TAKE YOU WHERE YOU BELONG."

Turn back the clock 8 years, and Nguyen is vice president of finance for Mitchell International, a $600 million software and services business. As the company's FP&A leader, Nguyen was tasked with supplying key insights to management decision-making behind the sale of Mitchell to KKR in 2013. Meanwhile, 5 years later, Nguyen was once more in the M&A diligence mix when KKR sold Mitchell to Stone Point Capital. Along the way, Nguyen's M&A resume quickly expanded.

"At Mitchell, we were very acquisitive, and during my tenure there, we acquired 12 to 15 companies," says Nguyen, who frequently became charged with leading the integration of Mitchell's latest bounty.

In mid-2018, following the sale of Mitchell to Stone Point, Nguyen joined cloud treasury and finance solutions company Kyriba as senior vice president of FP&A. Roughly a year later, he was named Kyriba's CFO—a development that came on the heels of Kyriba's sale to private equity firm BridgePoint. There's little question that Nguyen's latest career chapter has a familiar ring to it and is perhaps part of a larger M&A volume that he first started creating 8 years ago.

Says Nguyen: "It's interesting how life can take you where you belong." ■

CFOTL: What are your priorities as a finance leader over the next 12 months?

Nguyen: We're taking proactive action toward making sure that our employees are safe. We ordered a lot of N95 masks and are distributing these to employees. We are shut down through November from a physical office location standpoint. We're protecting them from an employment standpoint. We're not trimming people's bonuses or salaries. Really, all that this means is that both from a finance perspective and from an organizational perspective, we will be ready to hit the ground running—fast—when we come out of this.

That's our priority for the next 12 months. Again, this is both from a finance perspective and from a people perspective. From a finance standpoint, it's about making sure that you have access to capital and that you can invest in the right way. I think that all of us are thinking twice about our past investments. Maybe now you come to the same conclusions, but you're going to think twice about them. You're going to be a little bit more methodical about some of the investments that you're making. We're doing this now. We're being a little bit more methodical about which direction we're taking when it comes to technology investments, real estate, and what's going to happen with this "work from home" environment. We think that this is going to become a little bit more prevalent. We've actually adapted very well to it." ■

SCAN ME

📱 TO LISTEN

THE REWARDS OF CUSTOMER INSIGHT

GUEST CFO
DAVID WELLS
ENDRA Life Sciences

Back in the mid-1990s, David Wells was a financial analyst for a Bay Area supply chain management company that boasted an impressive list of Silicon Valley marquee customers.

Nine months later, Theler has no doubt added a number of items to his list of finance leader priorities, but his articulation task has become far less daunting.

Counted among their clients was a large chip maker whose customer relationship upkeep had over time become Wells's responsibility. Because this was a coveted customer, Wells always sought to be highly responsive to any of the chip maker's requests for information, but he increasingly found his company's pricing model out of step with the customer's needs.

"There was a lot of confusion and a lot frustration over what the prices for our services and products should be. Basically, we needed a much more sophisticated pricing model that the customer would accept," recalls Wells.

Faced with growing customer unrest, Wells and a colleague created a new pricing model that was carefully tailored for the chip maker's business.

Says Wells: "It was very intricate and more specific, but it was modeled exactly the way the customer saw their business."

The customer quickly gave the new model a thumbs-up, and all was well—until roughly 4 months later, when Wells realized that the new model was about to deliver to his company a windfall that would generate 4 to 5 months of revenue within only 6 weeks.

"When I saw what was happening, I went to the customer and said, 'Listen, this model that we built ... there's kind of a flaw in it. It's a flaw in our favor, but we didn't intend for this to happen and we don't want you to view us as being unethical,'" recalls Wells.

To Wells's surprise, the chip maker was not concerned about the imminent financial swell of its purchases. It was instead highly pleased to have had a model created specifically with its needs and requirements in mind.

"What this taught me was that as a CFO you've got to understand the customer and you've got to understand your business," explains Wells, who believes that finance chiefs must first have visibility into customer engagements to better understand the inner workings of relationships with them.

He continues: "If you can distill it down into tools that will then quantify the activity, then as CFO you'll be in perfect shape to make the right decisions both for the customer and for your company." ■

CFOTL: Tell us about your offerings. What are they being developed to address?

Wells: What we do is to allow clinicians in their office alongside an existing ultrasound machine to tap the liver with a sound wave. We read the returning wave, and we can then interpret and help the clinician to monitor how much fat somebody has in their liver. Liver fat is a big problem affecting 1.4 billion people. The NASH field—non-alcoholic steatohepatitis—and nonalcoholic fatty liver disease (NAFLD) are a very big industry. There are many therapeutics, many drugs, with over 50 that are vying for FDA approval to address the issue.

Where we fit into that process is this: imagine having high blood pressure and imagine having the medication to be able to address that high blood pressure, but imagine not having a blood pressure cuff. So you would have no reasonable way to monitor whether the therapy or the lifestyle change is working. Right now, the only way that a clinician is going to know whether you or I have fat in our liver is to either do an MRI, which is very accurate but very expensive, or to do a biopsy, which is very bloody, very invasive, and, candidly, not something that you're going to do every 3 months to see how the fat in your liver is progressing. ■

SCAN ME

📱 TO LISTEN

HELPING OTHERS GET THE BIG PICTURE

GUEST CFO
ANDERS FOHLIN
Medius

E arly in his finance career, Anders Fohlin discovered that he could ratchet up his capacity to consume information and problem-solve simply by drawing pictures.

However, what had originated more as a personal observation would eventually evolve to something more as he discovered that his visuals could serve others.

"I started to regularly draw processes on white boards and paper to make things very visual for everybody and help others to get the full picture," explains Fohlin, whose knack for creating visuals and goal of making things more visible "for everybody" led him to begin viewing routine meetings as opportunities for visualization.

Says Fohlin: "I found that process maps and gathering people in the same room was a really good way to spark energy and collaboration and have people feel that they were important and doing something more than just shoveling coal."

Fohlin adds that his early efforts to create greater collaboration and inclusion ended up opening the door for him to various senior finance roles and eventually led him to the CFO office at software developer Medius.

Among the guiding principles that Fohlin says have influenced his leadership style and approach over time is the notion of transparency.

Ten years ago, while a senior finance executive at NASDAQ, he participated in a series of meetings to discuss the adoption of an activity-based costing model. "We would sit around the table and go product by product to explore ways in which we could improve," he recalls, "and this was done with representatives from all of the different functions."

Part of the approach involved sharing numbers more widely across the organization and downward to the workforce at large.

"If each employee can see the overall picture and what aligns their daily activities with the strategy and vision of the company, then they make better decisions," explains Fohlin, who adds that today—as a CFO—he's still drawing pictures. ∎

CFOTL: Tell us about Medius … what does it do? What is the competition like for these types of offerings?

Fohlin: Medius is a global software-to-service spend management company. We have operations in North America, in Europe, and in APAC. We manage transactions worth more than $150 billion every year in our systems, and the numbers grow quite rapidly. If you want to position us more clearly toward maybe more well-known brands, you could think of us as Coupa for the midmarket.

We improve the transparency and efficiency around source-to-pay operations. Think of this as organizational spend management: business-to-business costs, cash, and compliance. In the past, procurement and accounts payable have been silo'd in most companies, but today integrating these functions in an end-to-end suite supports operational efficiency, visibility, and control.

What we've done is to build modular solutions for the cloud. Our clients can choose whether they want to run the whole source-to-pay flow in the solutions or just individual processes—such as accounts payable, automation, or sourcing—and then expand into other solutions. One of the industry analysts who made quite a thorough analysis of our solutions called us "the world's best unknown spend management suite." I don't know whether that's good or bad, but we'll be a bit better known in the coming years. ∎

SCAN ME

▢ TO LISTEN

IN PURSUIT OF DATA'S DEEP IMPACT

GUEST CFO
MATT BOROWIECKI
Biofourmis

W hen asked what led him to open his latest career chapter as CFO of Biofourmis, Matt Borowiecki quickly mentions the 2018 sale of MassMutual Asia Ltd. to Yunfeng FG.

After helping to piece together a string of strategic plays for MassMutual, Borowiecki was instrumental in effecting the Yunfeng FG deal, which was a standout for the company and deemed by many to be transformational.

Having helped to spearhead the transaction, Borowiecki was subsequently asked to relocate to Hong Kong and lead international strategy and corporate development for the company. With his deal-making realm vastly expanded, Borowiecki might have been expected to rocket down MassMutual's transformational M&A track for several more years.

"I REALLY STARTED TO UNDERSTAND THE POWER OF DATA SCIENCE AND HOW INSURETECH, FINTECH, AND HEALTHTECH REALLY WERE TRANSFORMING."

However, the move to Hong Kong challenged him in ways that he had not necessarily anticipated. Seeking to discover new strategies for MassMutual to extend its reach in the region, Borowiecki frequently found himself in meetings with local Hong Kong venture capitalists and private equity firms.

"I really started to understand the power of data science and how insuretech, fintech, and health-tech really were transforming," explains Borowiecki, who found his career ambitions evolving and coalescing around the broader notion of making an impact on industries at large.

Knowing that his M&A experience would serve him well inside the start-up realm, he soon saw a new career chapter come into focus.

"Quite candidly, the exposure that I had to very different consumer patterns and thinking about health and wealth in different ways piqued my interest in the Biofourmis platform," explains Borowiecki, who adds that the basic premise of Biofourmis is to enable patients to compare their own physiological signals to metadata from a vastly larger population pool in real time.

Says Borowiecki: "We call them 'Biovitals'—they're effectively a real-time picture designed to help clinicians to predict and prevent serious medical events. For example, heart failure is one of our focuses."

It seems that as one career chapter closed for Borowiecki, yet another opened. ∎

CFOTL: What are your priorities as a finance leader over the next 12 months?

Borowiecki: With the exposure that I have had to raising capital in both public and private markets, I brought to Biofourmis some process discipline and experience with respect to raising capital and understanding that we were going to be raising capital sooner rather than later. I think that this is a helpful skillset.

Biofourmis is a global leader in digital therapeutics. We have incredible commercial traction. We see this in Singapore and Hong Kong and in the U.S. We have traction with pharmaceutical companies, with hospital systems, with clinicians, with patients. ∎

SCAN ME

📱 TO LISTEN

VALIDATING PLAYBOOK PROOF POINTS

GUEST CFO
JEFF EPSTEIN
Operating Partner Bessemer Venture Partners, Former CFO Oracle

I n the mid-1990s, when Jeff Epstein was busy satisfying the M&A appetites of media clients for First Boston, one of his smaller, but more boisterous clients asked him to join the firm as its CFO.

"It was the type of situation where if they had gone to a recruiter, I would never have made the resume cut because I had never been a CFO and I had never even worked for a CFO," explains Epstein, who was 32 when he entered the lively entrepreneurial realm known as King World Productions. A one-time family-owned company, King World had seen its stature grow inside New York's competitive media landscape as the firm began producing giant hit TV shows such as Wheel of Fortune, Jeopardy and The Oprah Winfrey Show.

"It was actually a small company with only about 300 employees, but they had three of the highest-rated, most profitable shows on television, with about $300 million of revenue and $60 million of operating income," recalls Epstein, who would go on to add consecutive CFO career chapters at DoubleClick, Nielsen (Media Measurement), and Oracle Corp., a mix that fortified his footing in both the tech and media worlds—but also revealed little preference when it came to company size.

"King World had been a family business that had only recently become a New York Stock Exchange company when I joined them, so I had to put in place some basic procedures, but Oracle had been around for many years and already had very sophisticated processes," notes Epstein, who today exudes as much enthusiasm for Oracle's approach to simplifying and standardizing its internal processes as he does for the entrepreneurial instincts of King World chairman Roger King.

"Three minutes from when an idea came out of my mouth, Roger King would have picked up the phone and be pitching our largest customer, " says Epstein, whose CFO tenure there lasted 6 years—a span of time during which King World would triple its value and ultimately end up being sold to CBS Corp.

It was following the sale of King World, that Epstein would open the career chapter that permitted his CFO career to grow beyond a single industry.

"DoubleClick was an early Internet advertising technology company and wanted a CFO from either media or technology, so I had the media experience part," comments Epstein.

Today, as operating partner for Bessemer Venture Partners of Menlo Park, Calif., Epstein marvels at the continued evolution of the two industries that shaped his CFO career:

"Two years ago, global Internet advertising surpassed global television advertising revenues to become the biggest media opportunity in the world—so if you're around long enough, you see some incredible things." ∎

CFOTL: What are the metrics you believe should be top of mind for those finance leaders looking to raise capital?

Epstein: If I'm the investor, I like to have metrics that offer proof that (management) has already figured out the playbook. So what are those proof points? Well, the first proof point is, do we have product market fit? Do I have a high net promoter score? Are a high percentage of my current customers referenceable, where the company can just randomly call a customer and they get an endorsement that the product's great. If I have salespeople, are 75% of my salespeople making quota? Metrics like that and which (validate) we have product market fit and we have a repeatable sales process. The other sales metric I like to see is CAC payback. If you take all the customer acquisition costs (CACs), marketing and sales, and you say how much gross profit per year I bring in from my new customer marketing and sales, does that payback in a year? Does that payback in two years, that payback in three years? At Bessemer, we want to see that payback in under two years. ∎

SCAN ME
TO LISTEN

PREDICTABILITY AND THE PIPELINE

GUEST CFO
ASHIM GUPTA
UiPath

hen asked to share a few of the experiences that he feels prepared him for a CFO role, Ashim Gupta recalls what he characterizes as a significant accounting problem. However, it was not the nature of the accounting snag that Gupta wants us to know about but instead how his initial response to the problem was somewhat clumsy and ineffective.

The event occurred more than 10 years into his finance career and did not lengthen the path to his next promotion because he had only just arrived in a new role as a divisional CFO for GE Water, a General Electric Corp. operating unit specializing in water processing solutions. Gupta remembers the accounting problem as being "the first thing to pass across my desk."

Realizing the gravity of the challenge, Gupta picked up the phone and called the more senior finance leader who was responsible for a wide swath of GE businesses, including Gupta's group.

"I was nervous about it, and I did not articulate the issue in the way that I should have. I didn't really treat it as a business issue. I almost treated it with some amount of fear," explains Gupta, who says that the uncomfortable phone call later led him to reach out to a mentor.

"He said to me, 'Your job is to help the business face reality,'" recalls Gupta, remembering the words of his mentor. In short, the mentor told him that the senior finance leader wanted facts and not fear.

"I had to learn through trial by fire, and I failed the first time," admits Gupta, who believes that finance executives must be keenly aware of the facts when delivering bad news and seek to expose possible avenues to where a solution can potentially take root. ■

CFOTL: What are your priorities as a finance leader over the next twelve months?

Gupta: When it comes to pipeline ... I would say we've done a great job of becoming good at the current quarter. We need to be good as a finance team at understanding and influencing the next two or three quarters. ... Do we understand what our pipeline is? Do we understand our customers' buying behaviors so that we can model and predict things efficiently? That's kind of one really big priority for me. The second one is around data science and the digital environment. In our company, we don't have hundreds of years of data pent up that we can put to (work) ... Building the foundation of a truly integrated data environment to feed automation and to inform us on a real time basis is an important priority. This means more than just a fancy dashboard. That is true actionable information and using data science to help us be predictive, allowing us to understand the correlation of different variables.

"OVER THE NEXT YEAR, PEOPLE WILL START ASKING, 'OKAY, WHAT'S MY NEXT STEP? HOW DO I GROW? HOW DO I DEVELOP?' AT GENERAL ELECTRIC, THAT WAS INGRAINED IN THE SYSTEM."

And then the third priority is a little bit more mundane. It's career paths. I would say being a new organization, our average tenure at UiPath for employees in finance, maybe nine months or 10 months. Over the next year, people will start asking, "Okay, what's my next step? How do I grow? How do I develop?" At General Electric, that was ingrained in the system. ■

SCAN ME

▢ TO LISTEN

FINDING YOUR SEAT AT THE M&A TABLE

GUEST CFO
DENNIS MCGRATH
PAVmed

ennis McGrath was only recently married and a new home owner when he was invited to a Phillies game by the CFO of AC Manufacturing.

At the time, McGrath was working for Andersen as an auditor of a roster of growing companies, among which AC—a maker of industrial air-conditioning units—was perhaps not the most glamorous.

"At the end of the night, the CFO told me that he wanted to hire me and would pay me a lot more than I was then making," recalls McGrath, who doesn't hesitate to reveal what allowed AC's offer to trump all other opportunities.

Says McGrath: "I went for the money."

However, what distinguished McGrath's AC career chapter was neither compensation nor, for that matter, a lengthy tenure (McGrath was controller for 22 months).

Adds McGrath: "It was not too long before the owner decided that he was going to sell the company and had a private equity group come in."

Still in his mid-20s, McGrath took a seat across the table from a seasoned group of private equity executives. "For me, my career has just kind of been perpetuated from there in terms of deal-making," explains McGrath, who has arguably occupied "the seat" from that day forward, guaranteeing a CFO career chock full of M&A deal-making. ■

CFOTL: What are the numbers you're looking at to make certain you're achieving all of what you need to achieve at this place in time?

McGrath: Well, that changes by the phase of the company you're in, right? So if you're in full scale sales phase, you're probably waking up looking at yesterday's advertisement success. And if you've got direct response, what of your revenues and profits were generated by the expense of marketing yesterday? We are essentially pre-revenue at this point with just launching these products. So all of those timeframes are measured by cashflow. It's what has my past been, where I stand today? What are my needs going forward? And do I have the tools to make sure the cash on hand meets those demands?

We have had an evolving sophistication of our financing activities from the early days of just the IPO and some preferred offerings with some unique warrants. We've had a rights offering, we've resorted recently to using convertible debt financing and that has been extremely good for us and extremely good for the investor, which is what you're always aiming to try and achieve in a balance. It involves a nominal discount to us, significant profit to the investor. Having the money when needed to continue to finance our business.

"EVERYBODY THINKS DEALS CAN GET DONE OVERNIGHT. AND THAT POSSIBILITY EXISTS. BUT I LIKE TO SAY MOST OF THEM TAKE ANYWHERE FROM FOUR TO SIX MONTHS."

CFOTL: Was there a hesitation on your part to move in that direction?

McGrath: You always carefully tread in areas that are either new to you or new to the business. And we closed that first tranche in December, 2018. We probably started those negotiations in that summertime. So everybody thinks deals can get done overnight. And that possibility exists. But I like to say most of them take anywhere from four to six months. I've got enough experience and generally they fall in there. ■

FROM COVID'S INITIAL SHOCK TO IPO IN 60 DAYS

GUEST CFO
DAVE JONES
Vroom

Not unlike the careers of his finance leader peers, the finance career of Dave Jones, CFO of online car seller Vroom, has been shaped and influenced by economic crises of the past two decades. Last month, as the initial shock of the coronavirus waned and the stock market rallied back, Vroom moved quickly to go public.

Explains Jones: "We consulted with our board and our investors and decided that the time was right." After pricing its IPO shares at $22, Vroom saw their value more than double on their first day of trading.

"THE VIEW AT THE BEGINNING OF CRISIS WAS THAT THERE WAS NO WAY THAT ANDERSEN WOULD BE TAKEN DOWN. FOR ME, THE LESSON BECAME TO NEVER SAY 'NEVER'."

This was not the first time that Jones had discovered a window of opportunity in less-than-friendly economic times. Back in 2002, he had found himself in a tight spot while serving as a senior manager for Andersen, the historic accounting house that collapsed in the wake of the Enron scandal of the early 2000s.

"The view at the beginning of crisis was that there was no way that Andersen would be taken down. For me, the lesson became to never say 'never,'" says Jones, who adroitly stepped from the ashes of the once esteemed accounting house into a financial reporting role at Penske Automotive Group, where he entered the CFO office roughly 8 years later, in 2011.

"I think that Penske was a $2 billion or $3 billion business when I first got there, and it was an $18 billion business when I left," recalls Jones, who prior to entering the CFO office at Penske in 2011 had served as CFO of Penske's European operations and consequently weathered yet another economic storm.

Back in 2008, Penske CEO Roger Penske had described the subprime mortgage crisis as "one of the most challenging periods on record in the automotive industry." The automotive company would post its first quarterly loss in a decade and painful personnel cuts followed, but for future finance leader Jones, along with professional scar tissue would come valuable lessons for the future. ∎

Q&A

CFOTL: Tell us about your arrival at Vroom, and what attracted you to the opportunity?

Jones: I wasn't the first CFO. There was a couple of legacy CFOs that transitioned with the maturity of the business. I think our CEO, Paul Hennessy, had done a terrific job over the 12 months before I got there of really building a fantastic management team that wasn't necessarily a startup team, but it was more focused on a public company team that could run a 20 or $30 billion business, which ultimately we think we can get to those kinds of levels. And so that was one of the things that attracted me. I was probably the third to last person in out of 10 of us. So I had the benefit of being able to talk to five others on the team and I knew that they worked well together. I knew Paul was building a good team and obviously I really love the space and it was just a tremendous opportunity. But yeah, I think my background as having been with public companies and plenty of experience with transactions of this nature was right in the wheelhouse for me.

Luckily I inherited a good team and we've added to that team over time versus changing it. Incoming CFOs don't always get that luxury, so I was lucky there. But yeah, it was building a team for the future. And then tactical things like getting four years of audits done, which was no small feat, so kudos to my team there. But it's always about the team. ∎

FINDING FINANCE'S CENTER OF GRAVITY

GUEST CFO
RAY CARPENTER
Xandr

hen Ray Carpenter retraces his steps to the CFO office at Xandr—an analytics and advertising company formed by AT&T's WarnerMedia—he singles out two earlier roles as having been outside AT&T's traditional finance track.

"I actually got kicked out of finance for that role," says Carpenter, referring to a stint as a marketer inside a start-up launched by AT&T's emerging business markets group. "We did things that were uniquely different from what AT&T typically does when it launches a new business," continues Carpenter, who in addition to marketing was responsible for the start-up's pricing strategy.

"I ALWAYS KNEW THAT I'D BE CLOSE TO NUMBERS, DATA, AND ANALYTICS."

Next, Carpenter joined AT&T's mergers integration group, where he helped to lead integration planning efforts for different corporate functions, a role that made him keenly aware of the integration challenges such future acquisitions as DirectTV would present.

From his stint in the mergers group, Carpenter stepped back inside AT&T's more traditional finance and accounting ranks and was soon named CFO of its Entertainment and Internet Services division.

"It wasn't a forgone conclusion and still never is. AT&T has a habit of moving people around," explains Carpenter, who mentions a number of different functional areas recently led by executives who in the past had held traditional finance roles.

Says Carpenter: "I always knew that I'd be close

to numbers, data, and analytics, and I felt that this would typically put me in the finance camp, but I wasn't surprised when other opportunities surfaced." ◼

CFOTL: Help us to better understand how finance is playing a strategic role for Xandr and how these business opportunities that Xandr is now pursuing have taken shape...

Carpenter: Here's a good way to think about it. The center of gravity, financially, for our business is driven by how we monetize advertising inventory that is associated with our DirectTV and video businesses. So when you're sitting and watching television, typically you're going to get 16 minutes of ads for every hour of programming. Well, the way this industry works is that programmers—so, think of any cable programmer—will ink an agreement with a distributor, like DirectTV, that says that the distributor can monetize 2 minutes of those 16 minutes however they see fit to help to compensate them for distributing the content.

What we've done at AT&T through Xandr is to take those 2 minutes and use the data that we have about our customers and the technology that we've built in partnership with a company called INVIDI to actually ensure that when you're watching your television and your program and I'm watching the exact same program but in a different household, you and I will see different ads, even though we're experiencing what would be considered a linear video experience. This is called "adjustable advertising." We lead in this area across linear TV providers, and it's been a great source of growth and advancement for the overall industry that is all part of Xandr. And there's a lot of technology and data behind making that happen.

As we built Xandr, though, in addition to this—and knowing that things are moving to a more digital format and more and more video is being consumed across software-driven platforms—we bought a firm called AppNexus, which was one of the leading independent digital advertising marketplace companies. We're now investing in how we stitch that together. ◼

WHEN YOUR PEOPLE MATTER MOST

GUEST CFO
LAURIE KREBS
Red Hat

I t was October 2019. Red Hat, Inc., was preparing to submit its latest quarterly results to its new parent, IBM Corp., and Laurie Krebs had just been named Red Hat software's new CFO.

As a senior vice president of finance for Red Hat, Krebs had worked closely with the former CFO and more or less assumed that the acquiring company would likely prefer to fill C-suite spots from its "home team" talent bench of senior executives.

In fact, Krebs says that during the course of her career she had never truly aspired to be a CFO: "I often wondered who would want all of that responsibility, especially after Sarbanes-Oxley came in. And then, at the time, I realized that IBM had just acquired us for $34 billion and that it was going to be up to us to deliver the results that were needed."

"I DID WHAT I ALWAYS DO. I SURROUNDED MYSELF WITH THE RIGHT TALENT AND STRONG SKILLSETS AND CREATED A TEAM OUT OF IT."

Krebs says that the finance team at Red Hat, like many executive teams within newly acquired companies, had experienced some attrition and was perhaps not as highly functioning as it had been prior to its acquisition.

As the first quarterly close for the newly acquired Red Hat approached, Krebs sought to reassure her CEO that she would continue to lead the team. "I'll help you out until you get a legit CFO," Krebs recalls saying—

to which her CEO replied: "No, no, no—we want you to be it."

The CEO then reassured Krebs that it had been a unanimous opinion across Red Hat's and IBM's leadership teams that she should become Red Hat's next CFO.

Still, the pressure was on, and Krebs had to not only deliver the company's first post-acquisition quarterly results but also activate the collaborative processes required to satisfy a giant parent company.

"I did what I always do. I surrounded myself with the right talent and strong skillsets and created a team out of it," comments Krebs, who says that her team today includes a seasoned "IBM finance partner" now tasked as sort of a go-between and translator for Red Hat and its parent.

Echoing the executive's words, Krebs relays his guidance: "Here are the deliverables that IBM's looking for. Here's why they look for them. When they ask for this, this is typically what CFO's look for."

Krebs adds: "He has been what I call a 'gift' on our team." ∎

CFOTL: Which metrics matter more than others for your business, and why?

Krebs: The metrics that matter to Red Hat as a stand-alone company are different from those that IBM as a corporation has typically focused on and from what their investors look for. Red Hat is a growth company. Always has been. Always, and hopefully will be for some time. The market is not anywhere near penetrated, and we feel that we're rightly positioned to help on this hybrid cloud journey. So, so much potential lies ahead for us. At the same time, IBM is positioned to take us on this journey. So it's a great marriage.

We are a subscription business, so we measure our results in single-year bookings and multiyear bookings, and we amortize the revenue for those subscriptions over time. This means that if things go sideways in a particular quarter, there are not a lot of triggers that we can pull to

SCAN ME
TO LISTEN

THE CFO AS ENABLER OF SCIENCE

GUEST CFO
IVOR MACLEOD
Athersys

hen veteran CFO Ivor Macleod first contemplated joining an early-stage pharma company, the condition known as acute respiratory distress syndrome (ARDS) was not appearing in nightly news headlines and was yet to be ranked as the number one cause of death among COVID-19 patients. Nevertheless, ARDS captured his attention—or rather, Athersys did.

The Cleveland, Ohio–based company, with fewer than 100 employees, met one of Macleod's foremost criteria in that the company was focused on the area of medicine known as "critical care"—a space that Macleod characterizes as having "high unmet medical needs."

"It was the science that attracted me and not necessarily the capital structure," explains Macleod, when asked whether he may have preferred to join a privately held firm instead of a public one.

"YOU TAKE BIG SWINGS AT BIG DISEASES, AND YOU ARE NOT ALWAYS GOING TO BE SUCCESSFUL. SO YOU HAVE TO BE PREPARED FOR FAILURE."

As the former CFO of F. Hoffmann–La Roche, Inc., North America, and vice president of finance for Merck Research Labs, Macleod knows better than most the risks being taken and the high rate of failure when it comes to introducing new medications.

"You take big swings at big diseases, and you are not always going to be successful. So you have to be prepared for failure," explains

Macleod, who says that he came to view "the job" of finance leadership in pharma as being one of enablement.

Says Macleod: "I didn't want scientists to be worrying about resources. I would take care of that. I had to make certain that they had all of what they needed to continue on their path."

Last January, when he entered Athersys's CFO office for the first time, he would have only a mere few weeks to work alongside his new colleagues before the spread of COVID-19 within the U.S. led management to encourage employees to work from home.

Suddenly, as the disease spread, ARDS began to garner headlines, and last spring, within a span of 6 weeks, Athersys was granted FDA approval for a COVID-induced ARDS study and subsequently began populating designated sites with patients.

"There is no known treatment for ARDS," comments Macleod, who appears to be savoring his role as an enabler of science now more than ever. ∎

CFOTL: Most of your finance career has been spent in large enterprise environments. Were small or early-stage companies always part of the plan, or was this an entirely new chapter? If so, why now?

Macleod: Well, my first real exposure to a small company was my present experience, Athersys, and Athersys is a very unique company. Yes, they're small, fewer than a hundred employees. It's a regenerative medicine company. What I think sets Athersys apart from a lot of the other opportunities at which I looked is that they're very focused on what we refer to as the "critical care" space. This is a high area of unmet medical need. The two leading indications are ischemic stroke and ARDS, acute respiratory distress syndrome, which both have Fast Track designation from the FDA. They have good data in both. ∎

SCAN ME

📱 TO LISTEN

RAISING YOUR ORG'S FINANCIAL IQ

GUEST CFO
SHANE HANSEN
Planful

W hen a new CEO is recruited to lead a Shane Hansen says that his business career often reminds him of the Choose Your Own Adventure children's book series, in which the reader assumes different roles relevant to each new adventure.

Hansen's latest adventure began last April when he stepped into the CFO office at applications developer Planful just as shelter-in-place orders were being issued across the country in response to the fast-moving pandemic.

"WE NEED TO BE ABLE TO ADJUST BUDGETS AND INVESTMENTS AND OFFER FORECASTS THAT ILLUMINATE SOME OF THE POTENTIAL PATHS FORWARD."

Interestingly, the backdrop of a looming crisis can be found in multiple Hansen career chapters. Turn back the clock 12 years, and you see Hansen working in New York as the financial crisis raged and banks began to collapse. Go back more than 20 years, and you'll find him working in central Russia as the Russian debt crisis unfolded.

There was even a stint as a micro enterprise consultant in Santa Cruz, Bolivia.

"Initially, I was pretty intent on saving the world," says Hansen, poking fun at himself as he shares the tale of a poor Bolivian shoemaker who turned his $100-a-month business into an $800-a-month one.

"This made just a fantastic impact on him and his family," explains Hansen, who notes that the cobbler was one of 10 small businesses to which Hansen's team of consultants tried to teach the virtues of abiding by some simple business principles. "We introduced them to a few basic precepts like 'Don't eat up your inventory' and 'Don't spend more than you make,'" comments Hansen, who adds that he now expects to put similar principles to work at Planful. ■

CFOTL: Having only stepped in to the CFO office in April, what is the vision you have for the role of CFO?

Hansen: I'm really keen on having Planful be a world class FP&A organization and definitely be one of the best users of the Planful platform. I think that's important for us as an organization to eat our own cooking so to speak. On the second initiative of covering the basics, particularly in times like these where there's high level of uncertainty, we need to be able to iterate on company plans and department plans. We need to be able to adjust budgets and investments and offer forecasts that illuminate some of the potential paths forward. So I'm talking about basic competencies here like a direct method cashflow forecast that we really don't want to mess up. So that's what I meant by make sure we're proficient in covering the basics.

And then finally accelerating growth. I really want to begin with our end in mind and work backwards from there to uncover the activities that are critical for us to do over the next couple quarters. And maybe if I gave an example there, what actions would we need to consider to improve our customer life cycle or our customer experience that will ensure our customers are getting the optimal value from our platform so that we have low customer churn and a very strong platform to grow from.

...I believe part of the job of being a finance leader is to elevate the financial IQ of the entire organization. And I think we're seeing the role of the CFO in particular and the finance organization at large expand and change to meet that challenge. ■

SCAN ME

▢ TO LISTEN

WHEN AN OPPORTUNITY RISES TO MEET YOU

GUEST CFO
SINOHE TERRERO
Envoy

 hen Envoy CFO Sinohe Terrero is asked about his career chapter at Etsy, the online marketplace founded in 2005 and headquartered in Brooklyn, New York, he begins by explaining how back in 2008 Etsy's finance function was really just a loose grouping of tools and people.

"I'll never forget that I once had to go meet the bookkeeper, and he was like in Coney Island," explains Terrero, who says that the financial mind-set at Etsy during its early days was that data trumps accounting—or, to put it another way, that data was strategic to the business and therefore should be kept in-house, whereas accounting could be outsourced to Coney Island or wherever.

"Etsy was a marketplace, so the transactions occurred in big volumes, but we didn't send invoices. We didn't really have AR. Everything is paid by credit card on the Web," points out Terrero, who quickly became tasked with establishing more traditional processes in preparation for bringing the accounting function back in-house.

"Because of the nature of Etsy's business, the accounting function initially really didn't have to grow as much as the data function," says Terrero, who notes that even as Etsy's finance department evolved into a full-capacity function, the data mind-set still loomed large.

Says Terrero: "Understanding the transactions of the business on the data side was the primary responsibility."

Later, Terrero recalls, it was his focus on data and the growing volume of Etsy transactions that led him to back a strategy that not everyone was convinced was a good idea.

According to Terrero, there was debate inside Etsy over whether the company should be charging fees on payments received by sellers inside the marketplace. At the time, certain Etsy executives believed that the firm's mission should simply be to enable the sellers to sell more, which would then result in more transactions.

"WE ARGUED THAT THE FEES COULD BE A REVENUE SOURCE AND THAT, GIVEN THE VOLUMES WE WERE SEEING, THE STRATEGY COULD BE GAME-CHANGING FOR THE COMPANY OVER THE LONG TERM."

"We argued that the fees could be a revenue source and that, given the volumes we were seeing, the strategy could be game-changing for the company over the long term," remarks Terrero, who says that he was joined by a number of influential Etsy executives on the winning side of this debate.

Says Terrero: "When you look at the percentage of revenue that these fees now represent for Etsy, you see that they're actually pretty sizable." ∎

Q&A

CFOTL: Tell us about Envoy and what attracted you to the opportunity?

Terrero: I like to say we're challenging the status quo with innovations in a space that has long been neglected. Envoy has really redefined how offices interact with visitors, manage deliveries, book conference rooms. Now, with our new product that we launched because of COVID, that we call Protect, we're helping companies not only return back to the office safely, but do cool things like capacity management and many other (functional processes) that we will be launching soon to help folks manage their workspace. ∎

ACCELERATE AROUND THE CURVE

GUEST CFO
ALYSSA FILTER
Clari

When Alyssa Filter was named CFO of Clari, her strategic mind-set was the by-product of having been involved from early on in the development and growth of several of the Sunnyvale, Calif., software developer's organizational functions.

Having first been hired as a consultant when Clari was still a pre-revenue company, Filter discovered that she was less tied to the specific expectations of a job description than she was to easing the growing company's pain points.

Along the way, Filter says, she was able to grow with the company, and the more she took on, the more a finance leadership path became exposed for her.

"THE QUESTION WE'RE ASKING IS WHAT INVESTMENTS CAN WE MAKE NOW THAT WILL ALLOW US NOT ONLY TO COME OUT OF THIS BETTER, BUT ACCELERATE AROUND THE CURVE."

Filter recalls: "These weren't traditional finance and accounting projects. For example, I became involve in HR and sales operations, which required me to build new skillsets, dive right in, and get into the weeds in order to really understand what was needed in the company."

Filter singles out her early involvement with sales operations as having helped her to understand some of the unique challenges from the revenue side.

"At one point, I was even helping reps to create quotes, just to understand how the systems worked and what types of support were needed," remembers Filter, whose extra attention to the revenue side also served to sharpen her strategic sense around Clari's own software, a sales operations platform that promises to shorten customer sales cycles, improve forecast accuracy, and grow revenue.

As Clari's finance and sales functions have matured, Filter says, the two functions have been remarkably collaborative around commission plans, building quotas, and architecting the deal desk function.

Adds Filter: "We've built our teams around our strengths, so it hasn't been like, 'You own that and I own this.' Instead, we've said, 'Hey, my core team is really good at this piece, and your core team is really good at that piece.' What we have is a strong network of players on both of our teams." ∎

CFOTL: Tell us about Clari's response to the current environment in light of COVID's persistent presence?

Filter: When we were talking at the executive staff level, it's from a mindset of accelerating around the curve. And so I think our CEO has really coined that phrase, but that's the lens that we're looking through and the question we're asking is what investments can we make now that will allow us not only to come out of this better, but accelerate around the curve. And allow us when we have changes in the macro environment to be tremendously successful.

...We just hired a Chief People Officer, but until three months ago, I was also leading the HR teams as well. In the current environment, human capital is more important than ever. And so (as we consider) our response to the current environment, and one of the most important things that we had to evaluate and really understand is where to place our bets on people. ∎

SCAN ME

📱 TO LISTEN

THE PATH TO GREATER PROFITS

GUEST CFO
JASON PETERSON
EPAM SYSTEMS, INC.

When asked to share an experience or two that prepared him for a finance leadership role, Jason Peterson recalls an early lesson he received not from a controller, FP&A leader, or CFO, but from a group of engineers.

According to Peterson, his company at the time did not operate as cross-functionally as many firms do today, a situation that very often led business functions to focus almost exclusively on their own goals and priorities, with little inclination toward cross-functional collaboration.

"PEOPLE IN THE FINANCE FUNCTION WOULD SAY, 'ENGINEERS! THEY DON'T CARE ABOUT THE BUSINESS... THEY JUST WANT TO PRODUCE AN ELEGANT SOLUTION."

"Oftentimes, people in the finance function would say, 'Engineers! They don't care about the business. They don't really want to drive revenues, and they don't care how much things cost. They just want to produce an elegant solution,'" explains Peterson, who says that there finally came a day when he decided to turn his back on the finance team's conventional wisdom regarding engineers and begin to supply the engineering team with more management numbers.

"What I realized was that if you actually gave them a little bit of a road map as to how they could accomplish what they really wanted to accomplish and then supported them with what I would call generally high-quality management reporting, you could

actually get an excellent outcome," comments Peterson, who notes that his efforts to educate engineers drove down the company's "bill of materials" costs while improving the gross margins on multiple products.

Today, as CFO of EPAM Systems, Peterson appears to have this early lesson top-of-mind as he seeks to increase awareness across the organization of what impacts profitability.

Says Peterson: "Once we made certain that we were able to report the types of information that were driving changes in profitability, we then made certain that the company understood what the drivers were." It's enough to grab even an engineer's attention. ■

CFOTL: You first arrived at EPAM in 2017, can you tell us what was top of mind as you entered the office? What were some of your early priorities?

Peterson: I joined a company that was growing rapidly, that's got pretty solid profitability in it, a pretty capable finance organization. You kind of look under the hood and what you're trying to do is make improvements without breaking anything. One of the things that happened is, the company had grown really quickly. And I think over a period of time sometimes you'll under-invest in certain functions and I think that was probably the case with finance.

I started by making some strategic hires, so strengthen the external reporting, the controllership and the tax schemes. And then from a reorganization standpoint, I've done a lot of things, but much of my career has been in FP&A, so I work with a head of FP&A who already had some ideas. When we organized the FP&A group, to not only support corporate leadership decisions, but to be able to take information, decision making down to the BU level and be more supportive of the different business units while of course continuing to support the senior leadership. ■

SCAN ME

📱 TO LISTEN

LEARNING THE LYRICS TO A FINANCE CAREER

GUEST CFO
MARK SARGENT
Westhaven Power

t the start of his finance career, Mark Sargent says, he could not picture himself working for a large, big-name corporation. He says that he was drawn instead to smaller companies, which he believed would be more accepting of "creative types" or those employees more prone to self-expression.

In Sargent's case, an accounting and finance job was Plan B, or a "safety" occupation in case his aspirations to become a rock musician didn't pan out.

Interestingly, it was Sargent's deliberate avoidance of big business that undoubtedly allowed him to quickly garner some of the experiences that finance career builders long to add to their resumes.

"The very first job that I got was really a perfect fit: It was a small paper-making company, and I quickly learned that they were 9 months away from an IPO," recalls Sargent, who was hired as a cost accountant but quickly found himself reassigned to oversee the implementation of a new accounting system intended to add some muscle to the company's post-IPO reporting regimen.

This was the type of early career experience that later helped Sargent to open the door to more senior finance and accounting roles, such as the operations controller post he took on at Spectrian, a Sunnyvale, Calif., technology company. After years of serving government and aerospace industry customers, Spectrian, in the mid-1990s, moved to supply its cellular technology offerings to commercial customers in light of the growing infrastructure opportunities driven by cellular phone usage.

Not unlike had occurred in Sargent's first career chapter, Spectrian went public within months of his arrival, increasing the demand for improved visibility into the numbers and challenging the finance team to routinely produce metrics that could help management to better set performance expectations. "I really consider it my inflection point in becoming a CFO and a leader," explains Sargent, who adds that it was his breadth of visibility across the company and his awareness of being part of a team of highly skilled finance professionals that whetted his appetite for more and turned his finance career into Plan A. ■

Sargent: One of the things that's unique about Westhaven and that attracted me was that at its core it is a trade company. By "trade," I mean the construction trades, electrical, roofing, HVAC, and so on, and that's really where it's rooted.

"WHAT INTERESTED ME... WAS THE PROSPECT OF THE COMPANY BECOMING LESS OF A CONTRACTOR AND MORE OF A NEXT-GENERATION POWER COMPANY. "

In 2011, the company started to add solar installations to its profile of products, and this has led to some pretty good success over time. What interested me in 2018, when I joined, was the prospect of the company becoming less of a contractor and more of a next-generation power company. In fact, we just recently changed our DBA to Westhaven Power. We're bringing on new products like battery storage and backup generators. Over the next 12 months, the immediate goal is still to focus on getting out of the current crisis that we're in with the COVID pandemic.

SCAN ME
📱 TO LISTEN

Westhaven has actually done a fantastic job in weathering the storm. We made some immediate changes to how we went about business, and so far all of these changes have actually turned out to be even more advantageous than we thought. We're not out of the woods completely yet, so we're going to continue to be very diligent in everything that we need to do to finish off this passage through the pandemic. ■

ALLOCATING RESOURCES TO ACHIEVE OUTCOMES

GUEST CFO
INDER SINGH
Arm

I nder Singh started off his professional life as an engineer, only to learn that the large engineering projects that he aspired to someday lead often faced as many financial obstacles as they did engineering challenges.

So, Singh says, he went back to school and earned an MBA in finance, allowing him to redirect his career down a path populated with unique and imaginative financing deals to support engineering feats as well as business transformations.

"OTHER COMPANIES WERE JUST OFFERING TYPICAL BANK FINANCING. IN OUR CASE, WE SAID, 'LET'S DO AN OIL BARTER AGREEMENT.'"

One of the more innovative financing projects that Singh has helped to champion came along in the 1990s, when he was working as a business development executive for AT&T Corp. It seems that the Kingdom of Saudi Arabia was looking to upgrade its telecommunications infrastructure—to the tune of $4 billion.

"Other companies were just offering typical bank financing. In our case, we said, 'Let's do an oil barter agreement,'" explains Singh, who says that the proposal involved having Saudi Arabia supply $4 billion of oil to Chevron Corp., which then would pay $4 billion in cash to AT&T, which then would build Saudi Arabia a $4 billion telecommunications network.

"If you just think outside the box a little bit, bring your engineering skills, and bring

some financial skills and common sense, you'll see what makes sense for three different parties. And guess what? We actually won the deal," comments Singh, who notes that the fact that Saudi Arabia may not have demanded such an imaginative financing solution is not important.

Says Singh: "The fact that we put it on the table made us stand apart." And so it goes for Inder Singh, whose imaginative approach to financing deals over the years has routinely set him apart from his finance leadership peers. ∎

Singh: Arm is, at its roots and in its soul, an engineering company. And it has to be that way because our product cycles are three to five years, not one to two quarters. So, we really have to put investments in place today to create ROI in the future. And so R&D and revenue don't happen in the same quarter, not even in the same year, maybe in the same three or five years.

So, one of the things that we've been really doing is to say, "What are the portfolio of investments that we need to make as a company from an R&D standpoint, for example?" What are the bets that are most likely to pay off? How do we measure that success? Where are we incubating new things that may take longer to develop? How will we make sure that we keep ring-fencing the right things, but also maybe reprioritizing and exiting some of the things that we don't want to focus on going forward?"

A big part of the last year or so has been, as we built our new plan, to say, "What do we want to double down on from an investment standpoint, and what do we want to lighten up on?" So again, that sits at the crossroads of strategy, as well as finance to say, "How do we actually blend the right engineering projects with the right financial outcomes?" And so you have to think of an array of different kinds of metrics. It depends on if the technology is nascent. Arguably autonomous vehicles are something that will happen over the next five to 10 years in a bigger way, and so it is arguably a nascent market. But at the same time, it is a market which, which is going to evolve from today's cars to tomorrow's cars. ∎

SCAN ME
📱 TO LISTEN

EXERCISING DISCIPLINE TO EXPOSE TREND LINES

GUEST CFO
ANGIRAS KOORAPATY
ReversingLabs

When a new CEO is recruited to lead a company, it's not uncommon for the incumbent CFO to be replaced.

However, there are certain network-savvy CFOs who are able to muster enough influence with their boards to easily discourage incoming CEOs from implementing their displacement as part of sweeping the C-suite clean.

"THIS WAS A PIVOTAL MOMENT FOR ME AT THE TIME, AND IT LED ME TO DO SOME REFLECTION AND TO THINK ABOUT MY CAREER."

Angiras Koorapaty was not one of these well-connected CFOs. Or at least he wasn't about 20 years ago, when he found himself forfeiting a finance leadership position to a newly arrived CEO's CFO pick.

"This was a pivotal moment for me at the time, and it led me to do some reflection and to think about my career," explains Koorapaty, who says that he later realized that as a CFO he had been too focused on the company's internal operations and had failed to build important relationships with board members, investors, and other stakeholders.

Says Koorapaty: "As a result, there was a change in finance leadership."

The eviction prompted Koorapaty to take action. Eager to put the experience behind him and open the door to new opportunities, he began working with

a business coach, an advisor who specialized in coaching CEOs but understood the CFO role well.

Koorapaty says that he personally "set the agenda" and identified the areas that he wanted to address—but that the coach held him accountable.

"Oftentimes, I found him to be a pain in the neck. I did not always look forward to our calls, but I stuck with them. This made me a better CFO and a better partner for CEOs, and—most important—it made me a better communicator with my boards and a better relationship builder," he explains.

Several CFO tours of duty later, Koorapaty is now CFO of Reversing Labs, a cloud-based security and networking company based in Cambridge, MA. "When I joined the company, a number of board members approached me with their views," recalls Koorapaty, who says that he listened carefully before adding a number of items to his list of CFO priorities. For Koorapaty, better communication begins with listening. ■

CFOTL: Can you help us to better understand the types of opportunities that you are trying to measure?

Koorapaty: When we talk about opportunities, these are basically sales opportunities, which are essentially a cascading metric that comes off of marketing qualified leads. There's kind of a handoff that happens between marketing and sales. Once there's an opportunity that's been established, your sales pipeline journey begins. It is extremely important to be able to accurately measure and track these opportunities and the dollar value of them.

I go a step further and actually look at the incremental opportunities or incremental leads created for that particular week. I share that information with the team so that everyone knows that this is something that we're laser-focused on. When we think about this on a weekly basis, it allows us to look at these metrics and see a trend line. ■

HOW FRESHLY RIPENED ON THE VINE

GUEST CFO
MATT HAGEL
Freshly

I t's a story that Matt Hagel likes to share as he networks with fellow finance executives and accounting types. Back in 2017—only days after stepping into a finance leadership role at the online prepared meals company Freshly—Hagel was reviewing the company's chart of accounts when he asked himself: "Why is Plant, Property, and Equipment (PPE) under Operating Expenses?" As he soon learned, this stalwart accounting acronym has long led a double life and is also used by various industries (notably healthcare and food prep) as a shorthand designation for Personal Protective Equipment.

Three years later, the protective gear acronym is widely known from coast to coast—just like Freshly. In fact, since its PPE entry first drew Hagel's consternation, Freshly has opened an East Coast kitchen and distribution center, an expansion that extended the firm's geographic reach from 28 to 48 states and propelled its sales to nearly 10 times their early 2017 volumes.

"I inherited a finance and accounting team of three, and now I have a team of 30," comments Hagel, who located many of his new finance and accounting hires at the company's three distribution centers, the newest of which opened in Arizona this past April.

"From a cost accounting perspective, we have feet on the ground, so if any issues arise, our folks can quickly step onto the plant floor and determine the correct inventory number or provide whatever other information is needed," says Hagel, who entered 2020 keen to sharpen his team's focus on costs after years of marshaling resources and new plant capacity to accommodate growth.

Then COVID arrived. There's little doubt that the pandemic has been an accelerant on the trend of consumers turning to online for shopping experiences like Freshly that promise safety as well as convenience.

Reports Hagel: "Freshly is focused on building the best company possible, one that will be ready for the public markets or remain as a successful private company."

Perhaps momentarily escaping Hagel's lines of sight is yet another option whereby Freshly is acquired by a giant inside the packaged goods space. Certainly, Hagel doesn't have to look far when you consider that Nestlé is one of Freshly's largest investors.

To be sure, Nestlé's move to acquire a minority interest in Freshly back in 2017 was somewhat out of character for the food giant that is generally known to swallow its quarry whole. At that time, Nestle was the lead investor in a $77 million round of funding.

Just as the pandemic has accelerated the shift to online buying, so too has it appeared to draw Freshly and its big name investor ever more close.

"This has been open-office at both ends. We have had a really good dialog that has helped us both to be successful," comments Hagel.

Back in March, Freshly engaged with Nestlé's human resources team as it formulated its COVID response, which Hagel credits with having helped Freshly to avoid the mistakes made by other food industry players.

For one thing, Freshly hired a number of health professionals to begin taking employee temperatures at every shift across its different locations.

"The words 'essential services' weren't even a term on March 9, and there was no way of knowing whether we would be shut down," explains Hagel.

As the pandemic bore down on different U.S. geographies, Freshly issued a press release announcing that Freshly and Nestle would jointly be donating $500,000 to Meals on Wheels America.

SCAN ME

📱 TO LISTEN

"What happened back in March was that there was a period of a few weeks when we had no new customers because there was so much demand by people who were already using our service," explains Hagel.

"People just needed more meals, and this transition to be more of a lunch solution is something that we never would have imagined happening this quickly," Hagel observes. ∎

BUILDING YOUR FIRM'S BUSINESS CASE

GUEST CFO
BENNETT THIEMANN
Applicaster

I t was the type of role that any recent business school graduate could envy—not because of the position's title (Chief of Staff) or how much it paid, but because of its proximity to management decision-making.

The job is one that Bennett Theimann remembers well as he looks back on the days when he served as chief of staff for the president of Gruner + Jahr's German magazine division.

"It exposed me to that sort of very-high-level strategic thinking. We launched magazines, we sold magazines, we bought magazines," says Theimann, who very often found himself finalizing some of the documents that Gruner + Jahr management ultimately used to brief its board.

"My job was to help senior management translate their investment proposals, budget requests, or whatever they needed to get done, and very often they needed money," explains Theimann, who adds that while the position was not officially a finance one, this early experience of being a "business case builder" later helped to propel him into a number of FP&A and senior business development roles.

Theimann, who would step into his first CFO role in 2005, has now occupied the CFO office for several early-stage companies, the latest being Applicaster, a SaaS developer specializing in app development and content distribution. ■

Theimann: What really attracted me to Applicaster was that I felt like it was a true product company. I really felt like the platform and the solution that they deliver had achieved a real product market fit. I was convinced after talking to everybody that there really wasn't anything else out there and that this was one of those rare breeds in the tech space where the product should really make a difference. We know we have a lot of companies that are tech companies and that there are a lot of companies that have good tech, and that's perfectly fine. You have competitors that have very similar and good tech, but there's not truly—at the end of the day—real product differentiation. A lot of companies rise and fall, last but not least, because of their branding or their customer success or their marketing or their financial discipline—all of the stuff that you would also have in manufacturing or in traditional industries.

"DO WE HAVE ALL OF THE COMPONENTS AND PIECES OF THE PUZZLE THAT MAKE A GOOD TECH COMPANY OR A GOOD SOFTWARE COMPANY WORK AND SCALE?"

I think that this was really the one thing that I found interesting. I thought that here was a product that really could make a difference or is different from the rest of the industry. That's what attracted me to it, as well as—obviously—that people like me don't get hired into companies if everything is hunky-dory. You have to know how to help the company to build for scale. I was attracted by the fact that there was a lot of my past experience—in media as well as in SaaS companies and software companies—that could inform how the company organized and developed its go-to-market.

Do we have the right size sales team? Do we have the right demand generation? Do we have all of the components and pieces of the puzzle that make a good tech company or a good software company work and scale? Answering these questions has been what the attraction is here for me. I don't want to say that it was a diamond in the rough, but for the purpose of this question it's a diamond in the rough, and I could do a lot to help polish and scale it. ■

THE BUSINESS REASON BEHIND THE NUMBERS

GUEST CFO
STEVEN SPRINGSTEEL
BetterWorks

Back in the early 1990s, Steven Springsteel nabbed an interview for a CFO role with a high-flying tech start-up. At the time, he was controller for Apple's worldwide manufacturing operations, but the buzz surrounding the brash start-up intrigued him, and the young but accomplished executive shortly found himself waiting to be interviewed by the firm's CEO.

According to Springsteel, his interview aspirations quickly became somewhat tempered as he sat listening to a stream of expletives originating from the CEO's office.

Within minutes, the CEO's door swung open and several long-faced engineers beat a hasty retreat, to be followed by a smiling and gracious Steve Jobs extending a hand to Springsteel.

"I've heard a lot of great things about you! Can I get you something to drink? Are you hungry?" Springsteel remembers the legendary tech innovator saying before explaining the role that he had in mind for the CFO of NeXT, Inc.

Recalling the interview, Springsteel says that he felt that he had just met with "the nicest, most charismatic guy that you would ever meet in your life."

Of course, Springsteel had reason to doubt first impressions, having for a number of years worked at Apple, where stories circulating about Jobs's darker side were plentiful. What's more, a book titled Steve Jobs & The NeXT Big Thing (Scribner, 1993) had only recently been published, and Springsteel had made a point of reading it prior to his interview.

According to Springsteel, the text relates the experience of an Apple employee who was hired by a very gracious Jobs only to experience his darker side a short time after joining the company. Springsteel says that Jobs's evil twin was only one of several issues that led him to look for CFO roles elsewhere. In the end, he says, "I just didn't believe in the business model." ■

Springsteel: First, let me start off by saying that with every management role that I take there are four key operating principles that I run by, and I explain those to the team right upfront. The first operating principle is, never say no without giving options. It's very easy, particularly in G&A roles, when someone comes to you with a proposal to say, "Well, you can't do that. Sorry, Jack. I know you want to spend that money or structure the deal that way. We just can't do that." But you're not adding value when you do that. But, if you can now have that conversation with Jack, understand what's the business result he's trying to achieve, work with him on developing options, now you're adding value. So the first principle that I sell is, never say no without giving options.

The second principle that I talk about, is to think in terms of the business. When someone comes and says, "Well, what happened that our expenses went up last quarter?" Let's say I have an answer of "Well, we had a large accrual for compensation." Well, that doesn't tell you anything. Give the business reason behind everything. Look behind the numbers to articulate the story of what happened that answers their question.

The next two are open communication. My staff, we're going 200 miles an hour, but everybody knows what the other people, the other groups within my organization, are always doing. That helps because then you can leverage. And then very often, somebody will hear something that sales is thinking about a promotion that affects maybe some other groups within my team that they didn't know about it, and so

📱 TO LISTEN

that open communication is key. Then the last thing is, no surprises. Bad news does not get better with age. Let's get it out upfront. We don't like surprises. Give me an early head's up on things, and if I have an early head's up, then I can help you. Or other people on the team can help you get past this, and all of a sudden, what was the negative we can turn into a positive. So, I start off with those four key operating principles. ■

CONNECTING FINANCE AND OPERATIONS

GUEST CFO
JACQUELINE PURCELL
Deputy

J acqueline Purcell's path to the CFO office began inside an Australian law firm where as a young attorney she was advising corporate clients and their bankers on how to best address some of the legal hurdles that their M&A deal-making might confront.

At the time, her routine collaboration with different banking executives gave her a point of comparison to the seemingly less energetic legal world.

"They seemed to be having a little more fun and a lot more impact on the outcomes," she recalls.

"CFOS WERE VERY OFTEN THE ONES IN THE DRIVER'S SEAT FOR THE DEALS, AND THEY WERE JUST PARTICULARLY INFLUENTIAL."

"This is what sparked my interest in moving into finance," continues Purcell, who was soon headed to Stanford University for an MBA and then to New York, where she joined Morgan Stanley's M&A practice.

"I spent just over 8 years there focusing on a full spectrum of mergers and acquisitions transactions," comments Purcell, who says that it was during those years of M&A deal-making that she grew to respect the CFO role and the executives who filled it.

"CFOs were very often the ones in the driver's seat for the deals, and they were just particularly influential," notes Purcell, who realized that the CFOs across from whom she sat often applied deep operating experience to their decision-making.

Determined to add an "operations stripe" to her sleeve, Purcell would exit Morgan Stanley in 2017 and return to Australia, where she would step into her first CFO role at Culture Amp, a workforce management company headquartered in Melbourne. Purcell's appetite for operational insight has since led her to join Deputy, of Sydney, Australia, where today she resides at the intersection of finance and operations. ■

CFOTL: Tell us about the metrics that are top-of-mind for you at Deputy...

Purcell: As a finance leader, I'm obviously interested in financial data, but in many ways that tells you what has already happened in the business. I'm interested in the connection between financial and operational data and want to understand the connection in order to uncover what are the real, most critical leading indicators that are going to tell us where the company's going. That includes both understanding the potential to bring in revenue from new customers and also how the behaviors of existing customers may change, whether that's expanding with you or churning. I work really closely with our data team and, in particular, during the early months of COVID, we worked really closely together to establish what we called a COVID-19 dashboard. That was relatively operationally focused, actually, in terms of understanding the behavior of our users in the product and what they may tell us about what then would happen on our revenue side.

We're looking at things like the time between when companies are scheduling shifts and when people are working. We're looking at activity levels on the platform, how many shifts are being scheduled, and how many employees are then actually going and working those shifts. We're using that data to inform our forecast of what will happen in the business. Deputy is very much a monthly recurring business for the most part and really focused on our efficiency metrics. ■

SCAN ME

📱 TO LISTEN

MARCHING TO FINTECH'S NEW BEAT

GUEST CFO
MATT BRIERS
TransferWise

mong the more transformative chapters of Matt Briers's finance career was his 3-year stint monitoring and forecasting margin performance inside Google's UK operations.

"The core role was really to understand what was happening in the organization from a revenue and margin performance perspective and then help to operate the organization so that it could better drive that revenue," explains Briers, who says that his responsibilities included an unyielding effort to expose new drivers of Google revenue "even down to keyword searches."

"My role was to provide a hotline back to product in Mountain View," says Briers, who notes that UK customers are known to be among the most advanced users of Google's advertising offerings, outpacing users in the U.S. and other markets by as much as 3 years.

The insights gleaned by Briers and his team would become an important strategic voice for both sales and finance at Google and allowed Briers to add an impressive FP&A chapter to a career that up until Google might have advanced in any number of directions.

Still, his subsequent hire as CFO of TransferWise might have surprised certain finance career builders, given that Briers's pre-Google career had largely involved consulting roles rather than traditional accounting or audit work.

Today, Briers says, his consulting background has routinely informed his finance leadership as he helps TransferWise's finance function to sharpen its customer focus and collaborate across the organization.

Still, he admits that during his early days at TransferWise, his consulting past led him at times to too frequently focus on achieving "buy-in" across the organization. Eventually, he reports, "the two founders told me, 'Stop trying to achieve consensus—make up your mind and get on with it!'" ∎

Briers: In all my time in consulting, we spent a lot of time working with people driven by mission statements, and I can't honestly tell you that I believed in it back then. But since joining TransferWise, it's kind of this slightly religious maniacal focus on mission, which runs deep, and it's pretty amazing.

So my challenge is how do I help on this mission of pushing the product forward, such that we get faster, cheaper and easier, for a wide range of customers. The things I focus on: Are we growing? Are we getting new users? Are they putting volume through TransferWise? We know we're being used and we know we're useful if customers are engaged. … But when I say volume, the amount of money people are sending across borders, I worry about those metrics.

The second thing I worry about, is what's happening to price, so not just revenue, but price. Price times volume gives you revenue, but price isn't going down. Many CFOs might ask what is he talking about? "Why does he want about price and revenue going down? Surely he wants to drive this up?"

Well, actually, "no", because if we're going to be successful in the future, we know that we need to get cheaper over time. Because we believe it can be done and we believe it should be done and we can solve this problem of hidden fees that's equal to $200 billion and it gets paid to banks. So I worry about price.

Therefore the insight that we need to be able to provide to the business is: What is the unit cost? What makes up this unit cost? Unit economics as these (measures) have been called in tech firms typically. So we provide to every team on every route, what contributes each element of the unit cost and what are its drivers? Because everyone in TransferWise is hell bent on driving down the price. But my role is to make sure that we do this, but do it sustainably so they can drop price, but only if we can drop the unit costs." ∎

SCAN ME

📱 TO LISTEN

MILESTONES FOR M&A SUCCESS

GUEST CFO
STEVE YOUNG
Duke Energy

It was a little over 40 years ago when Steve Young first joined what would become Duke Energy, the giant electric power holding company headquartered in Charlotte, North Carolina.

"Not only has it been a long tenure, but also it is the only post-college job that I've ever had," says Young, who first roamed the energy giant's corridors as a finance assistant.

In the years that followed, Young says, he became involved in various finance-related projects as different executives sought him out because he had become recognized as a hard worker. One such senior executive, who sat inside Duke's rates and regulatory affairs realm, approached Young about a staff position in the department.

"It was a smaller group and outside of finance, but from what I could see, the group intersected with the lifeblood of the company's profitability and revenue streams and pricing," explains Young, who accepted the position and in short order acquired the regulatory executive as a dedicated mentor.

Says Young: "This person was a tough, hardnosed executive who had a reputation for being that way."

Years later, when the executive retired, Young advanced to his mentor's position, a promotion that firmly planted him inside Duke's executive ranks.

Along the way, Young's regulatory focus and experience afforded him a keen sense of how the changing legal landscape would alter the industry in the years ahead.

"I was pulled into that process," recalls Young, who says that back in the mid-1990s, he enjoyed a ringside seat as Duke pursued and acquired one of its early M&A targets, PanEnergy. "Mergers were rare in the utility industry back then, and certain laws had to be repealed—they were, and other mergers have since occurred," explains Young, who in the decades that followed influenced and championed a string of transactions that would reshape Duke's business over time.

"I found it a fascinating challenge to pull the pieces apart, put the new pieces back together, and come up with a cohesive business plan that was understandable to the SEC, regulators, and shareholders," remarks Young, who would find himself at the center of Duke's M&A activities in the mid-2000s, a period during which Duke sold off its international and merchant businesses and merged with energy company Cinergy of Cincinnati, OH.

"All of this happened within 2 years," says Young, who advanced into a number of organizational CFO roles during that period and was named senior vice president and controller for Duke Energy in 2006. He would be named CFO and executive vice president in 2013, following the energy company's 2012 merger with Progress Energy—yet one more transaction along Young's career path. ∎

CFOTL: Tell us about Duke's technology transformation practice and the role it plays in M&A?

Young: The technology side of any business, certainly at Duke Energy, is dramatically important and the importance is accelerating. And that's why we set up a business transformation capability. We've got a separate facility that houses several hundred people who are just looking at how can we take technology, whether it's data analytics or digital, and how can we put products in place that will streamline the efforts of employees in this company? And it's incredibly important. In the M&A environment, one of the big efforts that you do in integration is assess: What are your IT platforms for payroll, for work management, for benefits, for your generating facility, information for your financial systems. All of that. You'll look at where are your platforms? What are they? What condition are they in? Let's start planning the integration here.

One of the biggest challenges of an M&A transaction is the integration, where you get the systems up and running. The quicker you can get on a common platform, the quicker people will start speaking the same languages. ∎

SCAN ME

📱 TO LISTEN

FINDING YOUR FINANCE TEAM'S NORTH STAR

GUEST CFO
MARKUS HARDER
Contentful

T he Berlin headquarters of software developer Contentful occupies an old brick warehouse with heavy metal doors and broad functional corridors and spaces native to its industrial past.

Standing six stories high, the structure once accommodated its worker population with a miniature kitchen on every floor, a favorite employee perk perhaps first introduced by a coffee-loving tenant.

Still, not everyone at Contentful loves coffee—or at least its CFO, Markus Harder, doesn't.

"My secret is that I hate coffee—I just don't like it," says Harder, who shortly after his arrival at the firm put in motion a mandate to remove the small kitchens.

"It was arguably one of my biggest career gambles," says Harder, as he captures our attention and leads us to wonder why a finance leader would make a point of championing such a seemingly misguided decree.

Of course, Harder's actions are only Part I of a two-part tale. The second part involves the creation of what he dubs "a central watering hole" complete with a coffee machine worthy of Berlin's trendiest "third-wave" coffee shops.

"With all of these floors and their little coffee machines, we were never seeing each other—we never talked to each other," explains Harder, who reports that Contentful hired a champion barista for a 2-week period to teach every employee how to properly use the new machine to render an excellent coffee.

Says Harder: "Whatever you want to drink—a coffee, a latte, an espresso—you'll find that there's always somebody there who has been to the training or someone in line who is ready to train somebody else."

According to Harder, skeptics of the original mandate have largely been won over, but outsiders still find the coffee-making arrangement hard to imagine.

"Three hundred people, just one coffee machine— how does that work?" asks Harder, echoing the thoughts of coffee drinkers beyond Contentful's four walls.

"Well, actually, it works. And it's about the line. It's a social experience, and one that I celebrate each morning," remarks Harder, who says that on any given morning he'll spend a minimum of an hour at the café.

Says Harder: "We're all in the open. I'm available. Ask me something." ■

CFOTL: What are your CFO priorities over the next twelve months?

Harder: We're in the fortunate, but also tricky situation that historically we've doubled or more than doubled revenue over basically every year of our history. And that brings challenges toward pipeline generation. Because if you want to double the revenue again, you need to have a massively bigger pipeline. We are doing more with existing customers.

We're working with more with partners, and enabling them to be more educated with how to best implement Contentful. We're investing a lot in enablement and training and coaching. We have a Contentful certification. So if you are a developer, you can actually graduate with a Content-ful diploma. So I continue to invest in the team. I continue to invest in automation and systems. I'm actually accelerating hiring at this point and I'm getting Contentful ready to be a public company in a couple of years. That is sort of a North star. ■

SCAN ME
📱 TO LISTEN

THE REWARDS OF BEING PART OF THE TEAM

GUEST CFO
MARSHA SMITH
Siemens USA

 embers of Siemens USA's finance team would probably not be surprised to learn that when their CFO, Marsha Smith, is asked to reveal the experiences that prepared her for a finance leadership role, the ones that she relates most often originate from being part of a team.

Such was the case in 2004, when she had been assigned to a Siemens joint venture as a commercial project manager.

"I'll never forget: It was my first week on the job, and the project manager came up to me and said, 'Hey, Marsha, we need to ask for a change order on this one, so write a letter to the customer,'" comments Smith, who recalls thinking at the time: "I know how to use spreadsheets, I perform calculations—but I don't know how to word this letter."

Later, Smith says, she reached out for guidance from the technical team, followed by the legal team, before sitting down and writing a letter to the customer. Very often, the customer relationship would involve multiple partners and payment schemes, she explains.

"This was the beginning of my external-facing experience," comments Smith, who at different times during her career has found herself seated at conference tables flanked by dozens of customer executives and their attorneys.

Says Smith: "I'll never forget when at a certain meeting I asked a question and one of the managers asked: 'And who are you?'"

From her early customer-facing experiences on forward, Smith's business mind-set has become largely influenced by teams. "Everybody has to work together because everybody has a piece of the puzzle and we must make sure that we're collectively doing the right thing for the customer," says Smith, who believes that teams can also help to bring clarity to each individual's contribution. "You see who goes the extra mile," she says. ■

CFOTL: What sets Siemens apart today?

Smith: Siemens USA is a subsidiary of Siemens Germany, and globally we have around 385,000 employees. We're in 200 countries. The U.S. is the biggest market for Siemens. We have over 50,000 employees in the U.S., which is huge because Siemens is not necessarily a household name in this country. Yet we employ more people than many other very well-known American companies. We are in a number of different fields. We're in the healthcare industry. We're in the transportation industry—that's Mobility. We're in smart infrastructure, where we do building solutions, fire alarms, security systems, and various different energy-efficient systems for our buildings across the country. We have a digital industries branch, which provides software in the semiconductor space for the automotive industry. We have an energy arm with power generation and so on that's getting spun off right now.

It's really quite a vast conglomerate. Over the past several years, Siemens has been working to still maintain the Siemens umbrella and the Siemens name, of course, but to split off the operational businesses, to make sure that they can run their businesses as effectively and efficiently as possible. For example, Siemens Healthineers was IPO'd a few years ago. Siemens Energy is preparing for an IPO. Siemens Mobility, as I mentioned, was in the works to merge with another company called Alstom, and the European Union actually blocked that merger. There are a lot of different paths that the company is going on, and there's a big strategy to make sure that the businesses really are focused on the business and focused on growing their businesses. Ever since March 2020 and COVID, we have been very, very lucky that we part of everything that we do is essential business. ■

SCAN ME
TO LISTEN

THRIVING IN THE DEEP END

GUEST CFO
CATHERINE BIRKETT
GoCardless

Back in the early 2000s, Catherine Birkett found herself being pulled into confidential meetings where her company's senior management was discussing restructuring plans with the company's largest investor.

The company—a fiber optics telecom firm known as Interoute—was not yet 6 years old, but its days appeared to be numbered as the company sought to weather the telecom industry's historic collapse.

As Interoute's top FP&A executive, Birkett knew from the ongoing business plan's numbers that massive changes were urgently needed, and she as well as others were not optimistic about the restructuring options available to the company.

In fact, Birkett recalls, she and many executives had to tamp down the feeling that "this was not going to end well."

From a career perspective, Birkett arguably had less at risk than the other more senior executives sitting ringside during the restructuring discussions. Not yet 30 years of age, she joined the discussions knowing perhaps that other more gainful career opportunities were available to her outside Interoute's four walls.

Nonetheless, she had been given a seat at the meetings out of recognition of not just her ability to recite numbers but also her grasp of the intellectual property that governed the numbers.

"I owned the business plan," Birkett explains.

In the end, the company's multiyear restructuring allowed Interoute to find a new path to growth while operating under a new management team—one that included the 32-year-old Birkett as CFO.

"I was thrown into the deep end as a finance leader—I basically had to learn on the job," recalls Birkett, who entered Interoute's CFO office in 2003 and went on to serve in the role for the next 15 years.

"We managed to transform the company," says Birkett. Along the way, Interoute marched in step with a new private equity firm owner and closed a string acquisitions. Ultimately, the company was sold to GTT Communications in 2018 for $2.3 billion.

"Being promoted so young, I definitely made mistakes," admits Birkett, who credits her CEO and other members of senior management for standing behind her as she ran at breakneck speed to acquire the skills necessary to manage a quickly expanding finance team. ■

CFOTL: So tell us a little about your arrival at Go-Cardless and your priorities going forward?

Birkett: We had just closed our series funding around when I joined the business. So that was nearly two years ago. And that was about a $100 million that we raised at that point in time.

So we're continuing to grow and continuing to invest. And we're really excited about our opportunities in the U.S., because there is still such a large amount of business being done using check payments. We have a great replacement solution for check payments, because ultimately completing a transaction involves somebody's bank account, which is exactly what our (technology) facilitates. So we are just starting to build our brand over there.

Over the next 12 months, my goal is to ensure that GoCardless comes out of the COVID pandemic in the strongest possible way. And we simply must continue to help all our customers succeed. And then my final point, would be that I want to really continue to help push diversity and women in leadership. ■

SCAN ME

📱 TO LISTEN

THE PATH TO BEING COST SMART

GUEST CFO
JIM GRAY

Ingredion

 t's the type of business restructuring capable of striking envy in the hearts of many a company board member—and particularly those known to favor one oft-repeated bit of business wisdom: Never waste a recession.

At food ingredient maker Ingredion, where the recession's bite is directly linked to the eating habits of consumers, a 2-year-old restructuring strategy dubbed "Cost Smart" has begun to deliver on its cost savings promises.

In fact, in August of 2020, the maker of sweeteners and starches announced plans to increase its Cost Smart run-rate savings target from $150M annually to $170M—a $20M uptick that led certain analysts to believe now might be the right time for the food giant to step on Cost Smart's accelerator.

Not so fast, says Ingredion CFO Jim Gray, who reports that he already likes what he's seeing in Ingredion's rearview mirror.

"The opportunity around remote work environments and online collaboration has accelerated toward us," observes Gray, who over the past 2 years has replaced the dated architecture of Ingredion's finance function with a new shared services model and a mandate for greater online collaboration.

The restructuring involved the relocation of 107 finance and accounting employees to shared services location in Tulsa, Oklahoma, and Guadalajara, Mexico. The movement of this part of Ingredion's workforce is expected to be followed by that of a number of other functional areas within the company.

"This was not about lowering head count— it is about holistically redesigning processes to

have a lasting impact on cost," says Gray, who last month—along with Ingredion CEO Jim Zallie—briefed investors and analysts on COVID-19's impact on the business. After having experienced a significant drop in demand for different ingredients in April and May, advised Zallie, the company had seen "sequential improvements" in June and July as shelter-in-place restrictions had eased.

These improvements were more than likely first detected by a member of Gray's team, which had been working to expose how the pandemic is altering the buying patterns of Ingredion customers. ■

CFOTL: Is there a business dynamic that you are seeking to better measure, expose and alert others to in order to improve the company's performance?

Gray: Our business is global and the cost of our underlying raw materials fluctuates and we're also impacted by changing currencies versus the US dollar. So my finance team really works towards exposing that sales growth and the drivers of net sales growth more clearly. And we've recently updated our external reporting to highlight constant currency top-line growth alongside our reported. But I like to tie net sales and gross profit growth together. And in particular, in our business, when I'm looking at gross profit growth, and I think this exists in a lot of businesses, you need to separate the average, and you have some products that are going to be maybe lower price per ton and lower margin. And you have other products that are much higher sales price per ton and a higher profit dollars.

And you have to be able to de-average and be able to say, "Wow, if I just sell a little bit more of this higher value product, I get so many more profit dollars." And so, therefore, you have to be able to figure out and help the team see that, and be able to focus the growth on what we call our specialties business. ■

REALIZING HIS MARKET ECONOMY SPIRIT

GUEST CFO
TOM FENCL
Pricefx

T he son of two doctors, Tom Fencl recalls that while growing up in communist Czechoslovakia, to him a free market economy was more "an intellectual curiosity" than a possible career destination.

"When the Berlin Wall came down, I was midway through high school—it was a very formative experience," remembers Fencl, who says that the historic happening suddenly released "a market economy spirit."

After studying at Prague's University of Economics, Fencl says, he was "drawn to the big financial centers" and worked in London for 2 years at Stern Stuart & Co. as a consultant before heading to the University of Michigan for an MBA.

"From a university standpoint, the University of Michigan may not be the most obvious place for a European to go—but they found me more than I found them," explains Fencl, who notes that years earlier in Prague he had met students from the University of Michigan who were involved in a study of post-communist economies. "They were virtually the first MBA students that I had ever met," he observes.

From Michigan, he went directly to New York and Wall Street, where roughly 10 years after the fall of the Berlin Wall Czech-born and -raised Fencl became an investment banker.

"I worked as sort of a traditional investment banker, meaning that I covered everything from capital market transactions to M&As," says Fencl, who worked for Salomon Smith Barney (later acquired by Citigroup) and Bank of America.

"I left Wall Street just before the 2008 meltdown," he reports. "That was some lucky timing. I

moved back to my home country, the Czech Republic, with my newborn and my wife, and there I joined a private equity boutique," explains Fencl, who over the next 10 years migrated from what he describes as "transaction-driven" finance roles to more traditional CFO posts.

"I joined Pricefx in Prague—which was its largest office and where a lot of the banking office functions are," says Fencl, who was named CFO of the company in 2017 and subsequently relocated with his family back to the U.S.—a market that Pricefx now views as a primary source of future growth. ∎

CFOTL: What are the numbers or metrics that are top-of-mind for you these days?

Fencl: To remind your listeners, we're a SaaS company, or rather a subset of the industry where there's one metric above all, which is ARR—annual recurring revenue—and, more specifically, the growth of ARR. Then you rank companies based on where they are. For the past few years, we've been somewhere around 80% year over year. That's a pretty decent clip. Now, you ask, what did I change since I arrived? I didn't have to introduce this. They had already been told by the very first investors, "You need to watch your ARR growth."

The thing that I had to work on doing—and it was obviously a cultural shift—was understanding how to operate when using other people's money, when you're not governed by whether you have cash or not. When you have a lot of cash, the right questions are, How are you deploying it? How efficiently are you using this capital? The metric that I had to work on and make sure that the organization understands is payback—customer acquisition cost payback. Understanding the growth. How much did I have to spend to get this growth? This, of course, is something that then leads to further analysis because you break down the metrics into their components. You can't just buy the growth, right? You have to have a certain level of patience. ∎

📱 TO LISTEN

COMMUNICATING YOUR STRATEGIC PLAN

GUEST CFO
JAMES SAMUELS
EXUMA Biotech

amie Samuels still recalls some of the raised eyebrows that he saw after having completed in short order both the verbal and written portions of an exam that his future employer administered to job applicants.

Not unlike many of his fellow applicants, Samuels had been invited to take the exam after responding to a newspaper advertisement, but, unlike his peers, he had been the only foreign applicant—or, more important, the only foreign applicant able to complete both portions of the exam in fluent Chinese.

"At that time, my written Chinese was very good because I had only recently completed my senior thesis," explains Samuels, who first became immersed in the Mandarin-speaking world in the early 1990s when at 18 years of age he spent 12 months in China in a gap year before returning to the U.S. and entering college as a Chinese language major.

"Language is a tool to go do something else, so I spent a lot of my early career in trying to figure out just what that 'something else' was," remembers Samuels, whose stellar exam performance earned him a junior sales rep position with a Taiwanese medical device company.

"While I was good at sales, I discovered that it wasn't for me—it was too much of an emotional roller coaster," observes Samuels, who would remain in Taiwan but change companies as he migrated from sales into a corporate development role.

The job switch was enlightening. Says Samuels: "It taught me that my financial toolbox was lacking. My response was to get myself into the most quant-oriented MBA program that I could."

Samuels returned stateside and nabbed a Wharton MBA before being recruited by Johnson & Johnson to fill a CFO role at a small Taiwanese operating company.

"They don't give CFO roles to fresh MBA grads for nothing. They had an operating company that was in a little bit of trouble in Taiwan, or so I figured out after starting the job," confesses Samuels, whose career with J&J would last more than 10 years and span a variety of senior finance positions in cities such as Beijing, Shanghai, and Hong Kong.

Next, Samuels stepped into a CFO role for a privately owned manufacturer of air compressors. Based in Taiwan, the company operated six plants in the United States and Europe.

Finally, with more than 20 years abroad behind him, Samuels began considering CFO career opportunities back in the United States.

"When you spend as much time as I did in the Far East, you risk getting pigeonholed," says Samuels, who, as CFO of EXUMA Biotech, may have finally figured out what that "something else" is.

Headquartered in West Palm Beach, Fla., EXUMA produces cancer-fighting therapies largely developed at research facilities in Shanghai and Shenzhen, China—an advantage that Samuels seems uniquely experienced to leverage. ■

CFOTL: Tell us about Exuma.

Samuels: So this is an interesting and exciting company. The CEO is Greg Frost... he had an interesting idea, CAR-T, so that's using a patient's modified T-Cells to go and cure cancers. It's been very successful so far in blood cancers. Autologous CAR-T is hard to manufacture... So what we're trying to do is come up with a way to avoid the chemo, avoid the immunosuppression, and basically come up with a once and done injection where we can transduce the cells in six hours or less. ■

SCAN ME

📱 TO LISTEN

IN PRAISE OF PUBLIC MARKETS

GUEST CFO
STEVE CAKEBREAD
Yext

I t's not cheap to go public," concedes CFO Steve Cakebread, echoing the oft-repeated refrain that founders and CFOs confront when considering the prospect of selling shares in their companies to the public.

Concessions aside, it will come as little surprise to Wall Street and private investors alike that Cakebread—a seasoned finance leader who has taken public such companies as Salesforce, Pandora, and his latest firm, Yext—has come not to bury IPOs, but to praise them.

And 2021 might be the year when founders and CEOs are prepared to listen.

Certainly, few of Cakebread's CFO admirers are likely to question the finance leader's keen sense of timing. In fact, more than a few will likely be making room on their bedside tables for Cakebread's recent text *The IPO Playbook: An Insider's Perspective on Taking Your Company Public and How to Do It Right* (Silicon Valley Press, 2020).

"With all of the macroeconomic and pandemic issues going on, there have been as many—if not more—IPOs through August than there have ever been in the past couple of years," says Cakebread, signaling an optimistic note for U.S.-listed publicly held companies, which have seen their numbers cut in half over the past two decades.

The coronavirus, it turns out, might in part be the antidote for Wall Street's IPO blues. As COVID-19 spread, many companies made greater operational discipline and efficiency top-of-mind, which in turn led to the adoption of governance practices more commonly used by publicly held companies.

What's more, they began doubling down on culture, a trend that has prompted IPO-

minded founders to more thoughtfully expose the connective tissue between public ownership and social responsibility.

"Most founders want to create opportunity both for themselves and for the people around them, and this happens only when you go public," explains Cakebread, who notes that the social responsibility aspects of going public were a big incentive for each of the companies that he took public, including Salesforce, where he and CEO Marc Benioff identified a number of benefits.

"Marc and I talked about it a lot before we took Salesforce public. The discipline of going public makes your organizational governance better. It makes companies more socially responsible, and this was a big item for him and for me. It grows careers and spins off other technology companies," continues Cakebread, who joined Salesforce as employee #67, when the $17 billion company was eking out a quaint $20 million annually.

According to Cakebread, public firms operate with a certain rigor that privately held firms struggle to match—and VC-backed and private equity–owned firms can at times miss the big picture.

Notes Cakebread: "I actually find it tougher to work with VC boards because all they care about is the numbers. They don't care about the opportunity so much."

To Cakebread, the IPO process offers CFOs the unique opportunity to enter the ranks of visionary storytellers, where they play a more active role advancing the company's narrative and educating others about where the business is headed and what opportunities are being pursued.

"You're always going to have one number out of whack every quarter, but if the sell-side research people understand the underlying story, they can teach the longer vision to their investors and say, 'This is an upsy-downsy quarter, but long-term, this business is on track,'" he observes.

Cakebread cautions IPO-minded CFOs not to become too focused on the numbers: "What I have found in my career is that science and numbers are important, but you need a little bit of art to make a really successful bottle of wine or a really successful company." ■

SCAN ME

📱 TO LISTEN

BEING ACCOUNTABLE FOR EXECUTION

GUEST CFO
KATIE ROONEY
Alight Solutions

B ack in 2015, Katie Rooney was only 7 months into her first industry CFO role at Aon when her boss asked her to exit the office.

"He came into my office on November 1 and said, 'I'm retiring, and I want you to take on my role. I'm leaving in 8 weeks,'" recalls Rooney, who says that the news triggered a mix of surprise and fear, which she recalls outwardly expressing with the words "Oh, my God!"

Her boss quickly sought to ease her concerns.

"He said: 'You know what? It will be the best thing for you. If I stick around, you will never get the credit from the team," explains Rooney, who subsequently swapped her CFO business unit responsibilities for her boss's broader, divisional-level CFO portfolio.

"WE'RE NOW WORKING ON BUILDING OUT A DETAILED OPERATING PLAN THAT WILL HOLD US ACCOUNTABLE DAY OVER DAY AROUND EXECUTION."

Looking back, Rooney confides that she expected someday to fill her boss's shoes, but perhaps in 2017 or 2018—and certainly not in 2015. For her, though, the timing would turn out to be most fortuitous.

In early 2017, 13 months after she had officially taken on her boss's role, Aon announced plans to sell its employee benefits outsourcing business to private equity firm Blackstone Group as part of a "carve out" strategy that eventually rebranded the stand-alone business as Alight Solutions.

"We called ourselves a $2.3 billion startup," remembers Rooney, who says that she now realizes how her boss's decision to step aside in late 2015 ensured her inclusion in the early round of discussions that ultimately led to a deal with Blackstone and her subsequent appointment as CFO of Alight Solutions.

"We kind of had this moment when we said, 'The capital structure and some of the margin components just don't fit with the larger business,' so we started thinking about carving the business out," responds Rooney, when asked to recall the moment of insight that may have helped to hatch Alight Solutions. ■

CFOTL: What are your CFO priorities over the next twelve months?

Rooney: As I think about the next 12 months, we have to execute on the strategy we've now brought together. We are at this incredible place in time where our business is uniquely positioned to help solve the needs of our clients and their employees. We can help drive down the total cost of the workforce. We can try to drive and improve health outcomes. And as we think about the financial stresses created by the pandemic, thinking about overall financial wellbeing, there's so much opportunity here, and we've pulled the strategy together, and as I mentioned, I think we've built the right KPIs around it.

We're now working on building out a detailed operating plan that will hold us accountable day over day around execution, because it's about driving more value and taking an outcome based approach. We're leading with technology and really looking at everything, but we now have to hold ourselves accountable day over day to execute against that. And I think finance plays an incredibly important role there as we think about how we develop the operating plan to get all of our leaders, all of our businesses, aligned around what's required to drive that forward. So that's where we're focused. ■

SCAN ME
📱 TO LISTEN

THE VIRTUES OF TOP LINE GROWTH

GUEST CFO
SACHIN PATEL
Apixio

It's not uncommon for career-building executives inside the finance realm to obtain an MBA in order to pivot their careers in a new direction. Such was the case for Sachin Patel, who after finding some early success as a systems engineer at IBM Corp. began to study the path before him more closely.

"One of the things that you don't very often get to do as an engineer is to articulate what you did by using the written word or even verbally. Just having this not be a feature of the job was something that began to be evident to me," says Patel, who as the years passed found the laconic nature of engineering to be in direct conflict with his growing desire to play a more active role in shaping and influencing business strategy.

"I looked at two areas—investment banking and strategy consulting—and began pursuing both, which probably wasn't the best approach from a time management standpoint," explains Patel, who says that ultimately the numbers—or, as he describes it, "the common wiring between engineering and finance"—drew him toward the world of finance.

With an MBA in hand, Patel joined Citigroup and set about developing the relationships and industry insights required to succeed in the investment banking realm, until one day—roughly 4 years after his carefully executed career pivot—he received a call from a friend and business school classmate with a job opportunity.

In short order, Patel was accepting a director of finance role with Vantage Oncology, a network of cancer centers and supporting physicians that was quickly expanding across the country. Over the next 4 years, Patel would build and lead Vantage's FP&A team as he advanced from controller to the CFO office, where in 2016 he ultimately helped to sell the company to McKesson Corporation for $1.2 billion.

Looking back, Patel credits his years at Vantage for providing him with consecutive opportunities to prove himself as he climbed steadily upward. Still, he makes clear that his success there was not always obvious. In fact, even before he accepted the position, he needed to confront a potential obstacle that surprisingly had little to do with strategy or Vantage's financial footing.

"An interesting wrinkle was that I reported to the business school classmate who recruited me," explains Patel, who at first mentions his classmate to highlight the added rewards of having returned to business school but is compelled to emphasize the added complexity of such a relationship. "It was good that we had the baseline of a friendship, but sometimes this can lead to a little more ruffling," he says, before giving kudos to his classmate as well as to Vantage's management team for creating an environment where the two friends could both succeed. ∎

CFOTL: How has finance and sales collaborated in the past at Apixio?

Patel: We developed an in-house pricing tool for each of our solutions that we offer. And so based on our experience out of what the different components of the expense were, whether it's human time from the operations team, over to cloud expense that I mentioned, anything else that all gets folded into there, I should say, and then we can set the pricing based on that. And this tool allows them to check each of their contracts, or as they're negotiating they can check those margins using that tool. Ultimately, that goes to our chief growth officer who oversees that, and then if we need to make any additional decisions around that, we meet as a group. ∎

SCAN ME

📱 TO LISTEN

OFFICE SHARING ARRIVES IN THE SUBURBS

GUEST CFO
MIKE BROWER
Office Evolution

B ack in the late 1980s, Mike Brower's list of audit clients included a roster of oil and gas companies as well a local university and a number of different state and local government entities. It was the type of client list that any accountant based in and around Cheyenne, Wyoming, might covet, a fact made all the more undeniable by having Taco John's International top the list.

A restaurant franchisor with over 450 restaurants nationwide, Taco John's first began serving local Cheyenne customers in the 1960s, before expanding rapidly across the Plains and upper Midwest as it outfitted franchisees in small towns rather than big city locations.

"They just popped up everywhere, and I sort of had an insider's view," says Brower, who joined the Taco John's finance team in 1990 after having given notice to the Cheyenne office of McGladrey & Pullen.

For the next 6 years, Brower's responsibilities intersected with every aspect of Taco John's accounting and reporting function, eventually landing him in the controller's office, where he oversaw the company's financial statements as well as those of the 30 company-owned restaurants.

However, as time passed, Brower began evaluating other local opportunities and came upon an advertisement in the Sunday newspaper seeking CFO candidates.

"It was a blind ad, but you have to remember that this is Wyoming and everyone in the local business community sort of knows everyone, so I called the guys up and said 'Hey, I'd be perfect for you,'" explains Brower, who notes that the ad was placed by a fast-growing insurance company owned by two local

businessmen who had in fact underwritten policies for Taco John's.

"I told them that I'd love to talk with them about the job, but they were like, 'Well, we don't want to lose the Taco John's account,' so I said, 'Look, Barry isn't going to take the account away just because you took his controller,'" said Brower, while mentioning his former boss who at the time was Taco John's CFO. Brower got the job and became CFO of the insurance brokerage, which in short order began talks to acquire two Midwest insurance brokers. The insurance firm's appetite for M&A deal-making gave Brower a new set of experiences that injected some excitement into his first CFO role that even today he looks back upon and savors. ◼

CFOTL: Tell us about the opportunity Office Evolution is now pursuing.

Brower: Most of the country's workforce is at home right and people are finding they need to get out of their space, but they don't want to take mass transit downtown. They want to be able to go a mile and have office space available. That's what we're set up to provide for people because we're suburban based.

...We share a lot of KPIs with our franchisees, and the one thing that we've been really focusing on, particularly with COVID, are leads, deal creation, and the win and loss of deals at each individual location area. And we have coaches. We have what we call FBCs, franchise business consultants, and they're working with their franchisees every week. They have calls with them. How are we going to drive in business? How are we doing at closing deals? What training does your team require to help with close deals? You there is a big support for them.

Revenue is going to be a key word around here, and getting revenue back up to those levels that we had in March of 2020, which was a record month. So, let's beat that month and let's go forward. ◼

SCAN ME
TO LISTEN

THE INVESTOR CAME KNOCKING

GUEST CFO
GLENN SCHIFFMAN
IAC

here's little question that 2020 will long be remembered as a year of crisis for the casino industry.

Commercial gaming revenues in the U.S. were down 79 percent during the second quarter when compared to Q2 2019, a fact that made IAC/Interactive's August announcement that it was purchasing 12 percent of hospitality and gambling giant MGM all the more headline-grabbing.

"We think we found a once-in-a-decade opportunity to find a meaningful position in an iconic brand," explains IAC/InterActive CFO Glenn Schiffman, who says IAC's balance sheet remains flush with cash (more than $3 billion) after the recent spinoff of online dating site Match.com.

"CRISIS DOESN'T DEFINE CHARACTER, CRISIS REVEALS CHARACTER."

"We believe that Las Vegas will come roaring back, and this comes back to how IAC likes to invest: We like massive addressable markets with tailwinds from offline to online, and that's what we see with gaming," says Schiffman, who is no stranger to industries in crisis. Or so he explained when he joined us for CFO Thought Leader Episode 440.

Back in September of 2008, Schiffman was head of investment banking for Lehman Brothers' Asia-Pacific business when the firm filed for bankruptcy due to its part in the subprime mortgage crash.

Schiffman, along with other top Lehman partners, helped to manage the sale of Lehman's Asian business to Nomura Securities.

"In times of crisis, you have to separate the urgent from the important because in a crisis everything appears urgent but not everything is important," explains Schiffman, who says that he learned just how important being able to separate the two was when the clock was ticking in the wake of the Lehman bankruptcy and his team was seeking a resolution that would best serve Lehman's Asia workforce.

"We saved every single job in Asia—and that was 3,000 jobs, including my own," comments Schiffman, who adds that the Lehman bankruptcy, among other things, revealed how during a time of crisis an individual's character becomes more evident.

"Crisis doesn't define character, crisis reveals character," says Schiffman, who, after joining Nomura, went on to help establish and build the bank's North American investment banking division. ■

CFOTL: What does IAC's MGM deal mean for the company?

Schiffman: It's not just the online piece of MGM that, of course, is exciting to us. But it's the entire MGM Resorts business, including the offline hotels and casinos.

And maybe, it makes sense to take a step back and talk about that for a second. IAC has always been about rebirth, building, rebuilding. And this year, we spun off the Match Group. And that was a distribution to our shareholders of the 80% interest that we owned in the Match Group. And we effectively distributed $25 billion of value to our shareholders. And so in 2020, which is IAC's 25th year in existence, we're a lot smaller and our opportunity, our challenge, what's really exciting about where we are right now is, we get to rebuild IAC. And it's a great new moment. Now, of course, we have $3 billion of cash on the balance sheet. We have a roster of very strong businesses, three of which we just spoke about. So the question is, what do we want IAC to be? And what's the next journey, if you will? ■

SCAN ME
TO LISTEN

RETHINKING YOUR TALENT PHILOSOPHY

GUEST CFO
MICHELLE MCCOMB
Bluecore

J ust as Michelle McComb was imagining that she would shortly be joining another Silicon Valley start-up as a finance leader, the CFO of Lucent Technologies helped to upend her plans.

Back in the early 2000s, McComb's first CFO tour of duty was coming to an end with the successful sale of her company to a larger, publicly held software firm. However, within a matter of months, the buyer was itself acquired by the giant telecommunications player, and Lucent's CFO offered up a question to McComb: "What would it take to keep you?"

The coveted query is one that career builders long to hear but don't always answer in optimal ways.

"I packed my bags and moved to England, where I became CFO of one of Lucent's major divisions," she explains, leaving little doubt that her answer had landed well.

"I received tremendous international exposure as I traveled extensively and got to deal with finance people with very diverse backgrounds," says McComb, who worked abroad 5 years before returning to the U.S., where, over time, she has occupied the CFO office for a string of technology companies. The latest is Bluecore, a marketing technology firm that she joined in May of 2020.

Of course, in light of the pandemic, it's safe to say that Bluecore will likely be a career chapter unlike any that have preceded it, and, not unlike her CFO peers, McComb finds herself now being drawn to the mix of financial and cultural levers that influence Bluecore's workforce.

"I think that the people strategy—especially as we

SCAN ME

📱 TO LISTEN

come through environments like COVID—is going to be extremely important to ensuring how we retain and hire the right talent, especially when it comes to remote. What does the new office environment look like?," comments McComb, who begins voicing a series of questions: "What is our compensation philosophy today? Are we competitive? Are we a merit-based company?"

It's just such questions that in the wake of pandemic make McComb—perhaps more than some other CFOs—better prepared to land on the right answer. ■

Q&A

CFOTL: What are your priorities as a finance leader as we go forward?

McComb: I think it's super important that you have a solid foundation. So for me, I got to make sure that that foundation of my GL's accurate. I can close the books in a timely way. And make certain I have got audited financial statements. Those are super important.

And so for me, looking forward, especially in light of COVID, I think it's paying attention to the capital strategy. So around cash management investment, what do we need to look at? ...Should we look at acquiring a company or other companies? What do we want to do with our investments in our cash strategy?

So that's one side. I think a lot of times CFOs do tend to (focus) on capital and cash. I'm one of those CFOs who look at people as a huge asset. I also look after the people function at Bluecore and I think the people strategy, especially as we come through environments like COVID, is going to be extremely important to ensuring how we retain and hire the right talent, and especially when it comes to remote. What does the new office environment look like?

And then the last thing that I would say that I'm looking at is all around the other keyword that I mentioned to you earlier, around data. I think data is going to be absolutely essential in helping the company transform strategically. The decisions we're going to make, the avenues we're going to take to support our customers. So it's really double clicking down on the data side of things. ■

ACCRUING YOUR GLOBAL ACUMEN

GUEST CFO
ADRIAN TALBOT
Hotwire

W hen Adrian Talbot tells us that he parachuted into Thames Television in the early 1990s, the image of the London skyline—once used to brand the popular British broadcasting company —quickly comes to mind.

Suddenly, in our mind's eye, just to the right of St. Paul's dome, we spy a 20-something-year-old Talbot floating confidently downward.

Along with a boatload of first-class metaphors, this is the type of instant imaging that every conversation renders—at least for those of us on the lookout for them.

But Talbot's successful first jump—not unlike those of many future finance leaders—came about with a degree of serendipity.

"The lead auditor became sick—I was parachuted in for 2 years, and this gave me an early taste of media," explains Talbot, who at the time was an auditor for BDO. Several internal auditing roles followed, including one with Hilton International that required a good deal of travel in order to complete audits in different parts of the world.

"When you have chased the financial controller for the Caracas Hilton around the airport with a sheet of accruals or when the general manager of the Nairobi Hilton is yelling at you for telling him that he made a mess of a capex project, it is rather character-building," comments Talbot, who soon jumped back into the media realm with United Business Media, where he would serve as a finance director for the company's television broadcasting properties before entering the global communications sphere as a finance director for Burson Marsteller.

Talbot reports that years later, when he was

recruited to be CFO of Hotwire, a fast-growing global communications firm, he found a unique match—not because of his years inside media and communications but because of Hotwire's global CEO, Barbara Bates.

Bates had sold a communications company that she had spent 25 years building to Hotwire in 2016 and gone on to be named Hotwire's Global CEO.

"I was able to help her with my experience around the globe, and she was able to help me with her experience inside the USA," says Talbot, who today credits Bates with helping him to safely land inside a finance leadership opportunity. ∎

CFOTL: When it comes to customer engagement what are you looking at these days or what are you trying to now measure?

Talbot: I'm a very client-focused CFO, and I do actually spend quite a bit of time talking to clients. I often say I'm in charge of births, marriages, and deaths at Hotwire. So when the client arrives, it meets me, and when it leaves, it usually does.

And well, the marriage part, maybe not so much, but I think I learn a lot from the front end on those, and also from talking to clients. We had quite a lot of clients who said, "I don't want all this information, telling us where you've spent all the hours. I just want to know what you've delivered. I want deliverables, outputs, outcomes. I don't want to know where you spent all the time."

And I think one of the learnings for us, was to look at every office and strike higher minimum pricing. So what's your get out of bed price, and look really hard at things around that and say, actually, no, we're not going to operate at that level because the fixed cost of entry is too much.

The other thing for us is 60% plus of our clients we work with globally. So one of the key things for us is to balance the budget. France's budget might be different compared to the budget in New York or Spain. So how do we level that out across the organization and how do we keep everybody in our stakeholder group happy? ∎

[QR code] SCAN ME 📱 TO LISTEN

A LIFE SCIENCES ANGLER CASTS A STURDY LINE

GUEST CFO
BILL ADAMS
NervGen Pharma

I t's a familiar sequence: A strong-minded investor musters the will to lead and steps into the CEO office determined to revitalize a struggling technology company and put it back on the growth track.

For Bill Adams, this swift turn of events occurred only a year into his first industry stint as a corporate controller—a career chapter, he recalls fondly, that included a devoted CFO mentor.

In short, he would now be in lockstep with the new CEO as they together championed the latter's strategic vision that would upend the tech company's growing focus on software revenue and double down on hardware sales.

Or so the CEO believed.

"The challenge that I faced was that I didn't agree with him," explains Adams, whose in-depth knowledge of the business made him quietly question the new CEO's big bet on hardware.

"The company was full-steam-ahead focusing on software and system development, and the hardware part had already become secondary," adds Adams, who says that his broadened responsibilities within the company allowed him to reach out to different stakeholders and bring back "suggestions" to the CEO.

"Being able to talk to customers was extremely enlightening in terms of how to steer the company in the direction that it needed to go," comments Adams, who says that at the time the company counted Boeing and General Dynamics among its largest customers.

According to Adams, the company's strategy would continue to evolve as it lessened its hardware orientation and came to enjoy newfound success.

Even today, as Adams reflects on the circumstances that first advanced him into a CFO role, his sense of apprehension and excitement lingers: "I was not yet 30 years old when I was thrust into the CFO role at a public company, not really knowing where I was going or what I was doing." ∎

CFOTL: What attracted you to the opportunity at NervGen Pharma?

Adams: The key question for life sciences companies is, do you have the right technology that can be used in multiple indications? And would that technology be interesting for large pharma to take on and develop? And so, our technology is lucky. We're not a niche technology, we're not a 'single shot on goal,' to use a good old Canadian hockey analogy.

We've got multiple shots, it can be used in a number of different areas. And it's key to have a lot of opportunities because you can pick up the paper almost every day and read about another drug that's had some issue in clinical trials.. So to have the chance that you have multiple ways to approach it, I think is really important because you can't be all things to all people, but you want to make sure that if you go one direction, you can quickly pivot and move again.

I learned that from a company I had a couple of years ago and it was interesting. We had a drug, it was in the clinic for an HIV (treatment), and there was an adverse reaction. We had to stop the trial. So I remember I was at a board retreat on an island at the Chairman's cottage. And I had to try to do this from this island, trying to get a cell signal, to call our head of investor relations, to get a press release out before a long weekend, that we're stopping this clinical trial. And it was just the worst thing you want to do. Of course, the stock price tanked, but a couple of things, first: we had money in the bank.

And second: we had a very smart Chief Medical Officer and it turns out that the drug was really good at releasing stem cells from the bone marrow into the circulating blood, which is important when you're doing a stem cell transplant. So we developed a drug for that. And ultimately, the company was hugely successful. ∎

📱 TO LISTEN

ENTERING THE AUCTION ROOM

GUEST CFO
MARTIN NOLAN
Julien's Auctions

Had Martin Nolan studied engineering instead of accounting, his career path would likely never have entered the worlds of Marilyn Monroe, John Lennon, and Michael Jackson.

Still, Irish-born Nolan is quick to point out that it was a Green Card lottery, not his accounting degree, that facilitated his relocation to New York City, where he would meet and ultimately team up with Darren Julien of Julien's Auctions, the world's leading entertainment auction house.

Before the two men met, Nolan had traveled a remarkable distance from his early days in New York, where in the early 1990s—Green Card in hand—he had landed a job working at the front desk of the New York Hilton.

In the years that followed, the determined Irishman had networked his way up into a string of Wall Street jobs, where he found success as a stock broker and investment advisor at such firms as JP Morgan Chase and Merrill Lynch.

"Darren was doing a Johnny Cash auction when I met him—he was a marketing guy who needed a finance guy, so I joined him," explains Nolan, who met Julien in 2004 and the following year signed on with the auction house as CFO. By 2010 Nolan had become an equal partner in the business.

"When I resigned from Merrill Lynch in 2005 and told my colleagues that I was joining Julien's Auctions, there were looks of dismay—they would say: 'Why auctions? It's such a different business. It's so risky,'" says Nolan, who pointed out to his colleagues that the buying and selling on the floor of the stock exchange was no different than what takes place inside an auction hall.

Fifteen years later, he continues to wield a healthy appetite for risk, a prerequisite for any

CFO daring enough to enter the ebb-and-flow of the auction business. For Nolan, the risks are best hedged by using a mix of financial best practices and good humor.

Says Nolan: "Darren wakes up in the morning and checks Google and asks: 'Are we in the news?' I wake up and check the bank accounts and ask: 'Are we still in business?'"

However, there's one risk that Nolan may fear more than any other: that a finance career hatched by a lottery win could put Wall Street in its rearview and still someday be labeled as ordinary. ■

CFOTL: What are your priorities as a CFO over the next twelve months?

Nolan: I am excited about the future and our pipeline is very strong. In fact, my one sort of concern is that we don't grow too fast. That's the concern because we've had exponential growth in the last 12 months, and projecting out it looks to be phenomenal. I'm concerned about what is our optimum level. I don't want our business to choke us with so much property coming in and getting more warehouses and hiring more staff and sort of losing touch with the team.

I like being very hands-on as I am with the clients on the buy side and the sell side, but also with our team, because without our team, we are nothing. They are like family and we have a very good compensation package for our employees and very good health care, health insurance, life insurance. We have a profit share pension plan, which is almost unusual for companies today. They'll have some defined benefit pension plan, and we have a very good bonus scheme as well, so we really care for our employees because we know how important they are to the whole success of the business.

And so looking forward, we're trying to manage to the optimum size, we don't want to grow too big, but we are on a growth trajectory. So I'm training our (team), very competently, especially with the auctions that we have in our pipeline, and just trying to stay true to who we are. ■

WHEN OPPORTUNITY COMES YOUR WAY

GUEST CFO
KIERAN MCGRATH
Avaya

In 2008, as the economic downturn threatened to upend IBM Corp.'s financial well-being, the company's leadership was considering different candidates to lead a corporatewide restructuring when Kieran McGrath's name surfaced.

McGrath was known as a troubleshooter inside the ranks of IBMers, a seasoned finance executive whose 27 years with the company had produced a zigzag career trajectory—a long free-spirited path that signaled to IBM insiders that McGrath was both widely experienced and steeped in company loyalty.

"Early in my career, I got a reputation as a workhorse and a bit of a problem fixer, and while this was positive in the long haul, it did not always seem that way at the time," explains McGrath, who says that he was 10 years into his career with IBM when "special assignments" began regularly populating the path before him.

"I was constantly getting pushed out of my comfort zone because I was never able to stay in any one space too long," says McGrath, whose IBM resume included tours of duty inside the technology realms of storage technologies, semiconductors, and global technology services.

McGrath was offered the restructuring assignment, and, as usual, he accepted the invitation.

"This was really tough work because you're really forcing decisions as you try to push along a restructuring in response to economic realities," recalls McGrath, who—while in midstream of a restructuring gig that he hoped would last only 6 months—suddenly found himself being approached by IBM's leadership with yet another opportunity.

Says McGrath: "As luck would have it, the restructuring role became temporary because the CFO of IBM software at that time decided to leave the company for another opportunity."

McGrath was shortly named finance leader for the company's $25 billion software business, a demanding and high-profile leadership role both inside and outside the company.

"Clearly, I would never have been the CFO of CA Technologies or today the CFO of Avaya if I had not taken up many of these other experiences and gone down these side roads," explains McGrath, who would leave IBM after nearly 33 years in 2014, when he joined CA Technologies.

He continues: "This is kind of how I was raised—to be a little accepting of things coming my way, because there would always be opportunity associated with them." ∎

Q&A

CFOTL: What are your priorities as a finance leader over the next 12 months?

McGrath: From my perspective, it's all about sustaining momentum. We've had some very strong momentum here during the last three quarters of our year. Finally, we've returned the company to top-line growth. It's been a long, difficult road, and from my perspective, the journey is just beginning. So, #1 is sustaining this. For #2, I've been busy strengthening my balance sheet. We did some refinancing of our debt and restaged things, so we will be continuing to focus on this.

Organizationally, I'm actually spending a lot of time with my own function about continuing the journey of digitizing and introducing automation into our own financial processes. I think that we still spend too much of our time on inputting, retrieving, reconciling, and reporting on data and not enough time—certainly less than ideally in my own opinion—in really analyzing and using the data effectively to help to drive change in the business. This is some of the stuff that I'm partnering with my colleagues on. In both the IT function as well as on my own team, we really want to drive AI into our business. ∎

SCAN ME

📱 TO LISTEN

REMEDYING YOUR METRICS DISCONNECT

GUEST CFO
ROSS TENNENBAUM
Avalara

R oss Tennenbaum remembers that back in 2018, when he was a managing director at Goldman Sachs, he had conversations with a number of senior executives from Slack Technologies, Inc.

At the time, the fast-growing workplace messaging and communication platform was preparing to go public, and the company was making a special effort to educate bankers and analysts alike about the firm's business. As his questions became more pointed, Tennenbaum says, he noticed that members of Slack's senior management team would frequently permit other executives stationed along the conversation's periphery to supply the answers.

"At first, I thought that they served sort of a chief-of-staff type of role, but what I realized was that when the executive was pressed with a question, one of the sidekicks would always be turned to for the answer," explains Tennenbaum, who found his conversations with Slack to be highly informative.

Later, Tennenbaum learned that the sidekicks were members of Slack's business operations team, a cluster of analysts that he describes as being "cousins" to Slack's finance and FP&A teams.

"This team was incredible: They were so dialed in to the business, and they were partnered with Slack's executives, which allowed the latter to quickly make data-driven decisions," says Tennenbaum, who today, as CFO of software developer Avalara, is seeking to borrow a page from Slack and populate his own business operations and FP&A functions with teams of analysts on the ready to inform and supply answers to questions.

"This is about creating not just budgets but also operational plans that tie strategy and tactics to key metrics so that we can see when things are trending up or trending down

and be able to more quickly take action," adds Tennenbaum, who believes that many businesses struggle due to a disconnect between what he calls "top-level metrics" that are being widely shared and reported by the company and decision-making by "everyday operators" often situated deep inside a company.

"How do we make these people feel a sense of ownership of the measure and feel more accountable when it comes to driving outcomes?" asks Tennenbaum, who notes that a disconnect can occur even after a company has made an effort to push a metric deeper into the organization.

"What happens is that they don't do a good job of updating the metrics every month, reviewing them and quickly assessing where they're on and off track, and course-correcting," comments Tennenbaum.

At Avalara, remedying the metrics disconnect is now a top priority for finance.

Says Tennenbaum: "To me, that's the impactful part of the CFO job." ∎

CFOTL: What are your priorities as a finance leader over the next 12 months?

Tennenbaum: The background here is that Avalara is going from being a dual-product, U.S.-centric company to being a multiproduct global firm. There are a number of products and businesses that we have to support and direct in tax compliance, and we're growing rapidly. Then we take our customers: they're moving to e-commerce, and their tax solutions are only getting more complex and costly. So, at this time when we're a leader in the space, we're rapidly growing a large market and we're trying to support this business that is moving really fast and trying to do different things globally.

One priority is building out our finance and accounting talent to take us to a billion dollars' worth of revenue and beyond. We're at close to half a billion of revenue, and we're looking to go well beyond that. You really need the talent that has experienced a larger scale, knows how to achieve it, and can take you there. ∎

ACKNOWLEDGMENTS

We want to sincerely thank the 100 finance leaders whose profiles occupy the preceding pages. Without all of you lending your voice to an independent upstart podcast we would surely have fallen short of our goal of revealing in realtime the evolution of the CFO role.

Meanwhile, quite a few people that you won't find on the preceding pages, but nonetheless helped make them possible include Jack Burnett, Meagan Sweeney, John Herr, Jeff Epstein, and others.

Many of you became early champions of the concept of a yearbook profiling dynamic CFOs for this early support we will forever be in your debt.

ABOUT CFO THOUGHT LEADER

CFO Thought Leader is a biweekly, top ranked podcast featuring firsthand accounts of finance leaders tasked with driving change within their organizations. A recent recipient of the Excellence in Financial Journalism award by the New York State Society of CPAs, CFO Thought Leader is hosted by veteran journalist and editor Jack Sweeney.

Let's keep in touch – join the CFO Thought Leader email list to receive at no cost the latest insights and briefings from the CFO Thought Leader community at CFOThoughtLeader.com.

ABOUT JACK SWEENEY

Jack Sweeney is host and creator of the CFO Thought Leader Podcast, a popular Apple podcast and winner of the 2018 Excellence in Financial Journalism Award by the NYSSCPAs. A career business journalist, Jack is a contributing writer to *Forbes.com* and the former editor in chief of *Business Finance* Magazine (Penton Media) and the founding editor (and former editor in chief) of *Consulting Magazine* (ALM Media). He served as editor of *Integration Management* and Washington Technology (The Washington Post Cos.) Prior to the Post Cos., he worked as a reporter for CMP Media (UBM Media) in London. Jack lives with his family in Pleasantville, New York